Joy Breaks for Couples

Joy Breaks for Couples

Devotions to Celebrate Marriage

Dr. Larry & Rachael CRABB, Paul & Nicole JOHNSON,
Dr. Kevin LEMAN, Drs. Les & Leslie PARROTT, Gary SMALLEY,
Becky & Roger TIRABASSI, Dr. Neil Clark WARREN

WOMEN OF FAITH℠

ZondervanPublishingHouse
Grand Rapids, Michigan

A Division of HarperCollinsPublishers

Joy Breaks for Couples
Copyright © 2000 by New Life Treatment Centers, Inc.

Requests for information should be addressed to:

📖 ZondervanPublishingHouse
Grand Rapids, Michigan 49530

Library of Congress Cataloging-in-Publication Data

Joy breaks for couples : devotions to celebrate marriage / Larry Crabb ... [et al.].
    p. cm.
    ISBN 0-310-23122-1 (alk. paper)
    1. Spouses–Prayer-books and devotions–English. 2. Marriage–Religious aspects–Christianity. I. Crabb, Lawrence J.

    BV4596.M3 J69 2000
    242'.644—dc21
                       00-027522
                       CIP

Interior design by Amy E. Langeler

Printed in the United States of America

---

00 01 02 03 04 /❖ DC/ 10 9 8 7 6 5 4 3 2 1

~Contents~

PART ONE: CELEBRATING OUR FRIENDSHIP

PART TWO: CELEBRATING OUR IMPERFECTIONS

PART THREE: CELEBRATING FAMILY AND HOME

Part Four: Celebrating Our Oneness

Part Five: Celebrating—Even in Tough Times

Part Six: Celebrating Our Future Together

Part Seven: Celebrating Each Other's Gifts

Part Eight: Celebrating Romance and Passion

Part One
Celebrating Our Friendship

You've Got to Be Joking!

Les and Leslie Parrott

A cheerful heart is good medicine.

Proverbs 17:22

Do you two need a tissue?" a voice gently whispered from behind Les and me (Leslie). We were sitting in a theater watching a somber play when—at the saddest moment—something struck the two of us as funny. Hysterically funny.

You see, just at that moment Les found a withered old banana in his coat pocket. Who knows how long it had lived there, and he set this surprising discovering on my knee. Caught off guard by the incongruity of the banana and the play, I developed one of the worst cases of the giggles I've ever had. Les quickly caught the same disease. We tried desperately to stifle our laughter, but as we bowed our heads to hide our faces, we couldn't keep our shoulders from shuddering. An older woman behind us, thinking we were moved by what was happening on stage, offered us a tissue for our tears, which made us laugh all the more. When Les accepted her kind offer, I really lost it and had to leave the theater.

11

Just another day in the marriage of Les and Leslie? Not quite, but we do laugh a lot together. The tiniest things can sometimes set us off—an inflection or a knowing glance, a funny line from a movie, or a faux pas in front of others. We have the same funny bone and can't keep from using it. No wonder we enjoy our marriage.

Laughter does that. Any good friend will tell you that laughter is the shortest distance between two people—especially in marriage.

But from time to time, our humor is out of sync. Les has a small band of friends who don't think twice about busting him in the chops every now and then in the name of good-natured ridicule. And it always makes him laugh. Sitting around a table at a late-night dive after a basketball game, one of them might crack, "Hey, Les, we were all impressed by the spineless prayer you call a jump shot." Which brings the inevitable retort, "Yeah, it's about as good as the serious medical disorder you call a golf swing."

Well, it didn't take Les more than once to figure out this kind of humor doesn't work in our marriage. I say it's a guy thing. All Les knows is that nothing bonds buddies together like a little needless needling—as long as the buddies are guys, that is.

Humor can backfire if we aren't careful. But one thing we know for sure, laughter is good medicine for every marriage. Literally. Research has shown that people with a sense of humor have fewer symptoms of physical illness than those who are less humorous. Perhaps that's what Proverbs 17:22 is getting at.

But the benefits of humor extend beyond our physiology. The Bible reminds us many times and in many ways to bring the "sounds of joy and gladness" (Jeremiah 7:34) to our homes. Proverbs says, "The cheerful heart has a continual feast" (Proverbs 15:15). The psalmist sings, "Our mouths were filled with laughter" (Psalms 126:2). Isaiah exults, "Shout for joy, O heavens; rejoice, O earth" (Isaiah 49:13). Jesus told his disciples that after he left them, "your grief will turn to joy . . . and no one will take away your joy" (John 16:20, 22). The apostle Peter confirms that the Christians to whom he is writing "are filled with an inexpressible and glorious joy" (1 Peter 1:8).

So let laughter fill your home. And celebrate your friendship in marriage by lightening up and enjoying a good laugh together. Watch a silly movie with each other, share the Sunday funnies, tickle each other's ribs, play practical jokes. Or go to a play and yuk it up while everyone else is crying.

Father, bring laughter into our marriage. Surround our home with humor. Help us to experience the joy of finding something funny together each day. And help us to laugh at ourselves when we're taking everything—including each other—too seriously. We give you thanks for the gift of laughter and for what it can do for our marriage.

Absence Grows Fondness

Paul Johnson

After an absence of several years, I came to Jerusalem.

ACTS 24:17

Tonight I'm picking up my wife from the airport. She's only been gone for twenty-four hours on a quick business trip, but I've missed her, and I'm looking forward to seeing her (and not just because I'm a guy).

It's a little crazy to me. We spend twenty-four hours a day, seven days a week together. We're rarely apart. We joke that we usually are together unless one of us is using the bathroom. We travel together, work together, and live together (of course). Yet here I am, missing her. Crazy.

I've heard it said, "Absence makes the heart grow fonder." Why would that be? On some days, I just beg for absence. Internally, I'm screaming, *Get away from me! You're driving me crazy!* I never say anything, though. Then I slowly boil until I blow up, and we have a knockdown, drag-out fight. Makes for a lovely evening. We really want to be close then. Yeah, and I have lakefront property in Arizona to sell.

When children become snippy with one another, often one child is told to take a time-out. That child sits by him- or herself (we used to have to sit in the corner) for an "attitude adjustment" period. Or the child must go take a nap (which, to an adult, is a very appealing idea). Either way, the child is called on to separate himself from the group for a period of time.

Okay, so sometimes in our marriages we behave like children. We get snippy because of various stresses, and our spouse seems to further the irritation. Then we lash out and are in sore need of a time-out, for someone to send us to the corner or to our room for an attitude adjustment period.

Nicole and I get that way. A lot. In fact, before she left on this trip, we weren't behaving very nicely toward one another. But here I am, eagerly awaiting her arrival back home. Unbelievable.

In 1986, Nicole and I spent the summer apart. We both had finished our junior years at Samford University in Birmingham, Alabama. She was attending summer school at Samford, and I was working in Atlanta. We had been dating for a year and a half by then and had never been separated for a lengthy time.

That was a tough summer. We hated being apart. I would visit her on the weekends, but by late Saturday afternoon, a dull ache would set in over the thought that I would have to leave the next day. By Sunday afternoon, we were clinging to one another.

One Sunday, as I was leaving, Nicole came running down the hill from her dorm, crying her eyes out. My heart broke. I stopped the car, got out, and we just held each other and cried in the parking lot. Our biggest desire was for classes to start so we could be back together—taking each other for granted. We longed for the monotony of being together all the time.

It happens. Over time, the dailiness of a relationship settles in, and we take each other for granted. Things rarely change, and we rarely are challenged to see our spouse in a different light. We lose a bit of interest in one another, and we simply exist. But then we're separated for a period of time, or worse, a tragedy happens, and we instantly long for the days when life was boring, and then we wish we had relished those days more. In those enlightening moments, something happens in us that rekindles the friendship, the fondness, the appreciation, and the love for one another.

She's been away for only twenty-four hours, but during the day, I found myself thinking, *Oh, Nicole would like that.* Or, *That's just like Nicole.* Something stirred within me that caused me to appreciate her anew. I reconsidered how unique she is, and what she means to me. I fell in love with her all over again. Now I can't wait to see her.

I guess I should send myself to my room for an attitude adjustment more often.

Oh, Lord, may we value the gift of marriage that you have given us. Rekindle within our hearts, by any means necessary, the love we have for one another. Remind us of the unique place our spouse holds in each of our lives, and help us to express our deep appreciation and admiration for one another.

WHEN JACK FELL DOWN

Neil Clark Warren

> "Don't be afraid," Jonathan reassured [David]. "My father
> will never find you! You are going to be the king of Israel
> and I will be next to you, as my father is well aware." So the two
> of them renewed their pact of friendship; and David stayed
> at Horesh while Jonathan returned home.
>
> 1 SAMUEL 23:17–18 LB

All three of our daughters graduated from San Marino (California) High School, and I had the honor of speaking at each of their baccalaureate services. I was nervous, to be sure, because I couldn't think of anything quite so awful as embarrassing them by being boring or inappropriate—or by crying like a baby in front of all their friends. At the first baccalaureate, I decided to speak on what I now believe is the most powerful theme not only for adolescents but also for couples—the theme of friendship.

I focused my remarks around that grand old nursery rhyme, "Jack and Jill." I'm sure you remember how it goes:

Jack and Jill
Went up the hill
To fetch a pail of water.
Jack fell down
And broke his crown,
And Jill came tumbling after.

I took each of the six lines and related it to the graduates' life together. I think the same applications work for couples as well.

I started with the "Jack and Jill" line, and I talked about friendship's centrality in their lives. I ventured the opinion that the matter most on their minds that night was all the friends they had made in this place through the years—thirteen years for many of them. I imagined that they were both delighted with these relationships and deeply concerned about them. They were about to scatter all over the world for college, and these wonderful, comfortable, maybe even lifelong friendships would never be quite the same again. Still, the quality of their friendships represented perhaps the finest thing they had to show for their years together.

Then I talked about "Went up the hill," and I reminisced about the direction in which they had traveled together. I talked about the classes and clubs they had been in, the athletic teams on which they had played together, the committees on which they had served, the dances and the parties. They had indeed traveled together "up the hill."

"To fetch a pail of water." There was a purpose to their traveling up that hill. They had a mutual objective. They were growing up together, preparing themselves to be great spouses, parents, teachers, leaders, and contributors. Every last minute they had spent together had been related to that objective. Their years in school had been all about purpose.

When I talked about "Jack fell down," things became deadly serious. Theoretically, adversity is going to be a part of every life, but in one case after another, many of these seniors already had confronted adversity. Their parents had divorced, they'd failed a class, and a score of other problems had beset them. I warned them that adversity is always ready to strike; it strikes all of us at one point or another, and if we think it won't, we're fooling ourselves.

"And broke his crown." Suffering is horrible! The pain can be incapacitating. Most of these graduates knew from personal experience what I was talking about, and the others knew someone right then who was going through some miserable suffering.

"And Jill came tumbling after." This is what the old poem is all about. When you come up against adversity, when suffering is your lot, the greatest thing in the world is your friends' loyalty. They don't stand up there on the hill and wait to see what happens to you. Instead, they move right down into the suffering with you. And it changes everything about your life.

I wasn't satisfied that night to leave them at the bottom of the hill in a pile of suffering, so I composed a couple of new verses for the age-old nursery rhyme:

Jill and Jack
They went right back
To fetch that pail of water.
They filled their pail,
Came down the trail,
And loved their time together.
And through the years
With laughs and tears,
They lived their lives together.

For trust was found
When Jack fell down
And Jill came tumbling after.

At the center of a great marriage or a great life is friendship, and at the center of a wonderful friendship is the trust that develops when a good friend is there for you during your time of adversity and suffering. The friendship of your mate is something to celebrate. Whether one of you has tumbled down the hill and broken his or her crown, or whether the two of you are trudging up the hill hand in hand, you have someone to alternately laugh and cry with. And that should make every Jack and Jill happy indeed.

Dear God, thank you for our friendship. Help us to make wonderful friends of each other. Help us to remember what a friend we have in Jesus, and may his willingness to stay close to us inspire us to stay close to each other—in good times and bad. In his name. Amen.

WINE INTO WATER

Becky and Roger Tirabassi

*We who are strong ought to bear with the failings of
the weak and not to please ourselves.*

ROMANS 15:1

On the flight to begin our honeymoon, we were given a bottle of champagne as a gift from the flight attendant. We graciously accepted the bottle and placed it in our carry-on bag. This kind gesture from the airline wouldn't be considered inappropriate by most couples, but I had struggled with an addiction to drugs and alcohol up until two years before our marriage.

Neither Roger nor I mentioned the bottle after that moment, but I couldn't stop thinking about it. When we entered our hotel suite after the flight, Roger headed for the restroom. I quickly unzipped the carry-on bag, found and opened the bottle of champagne, and downed a few drinks—all before Roger stepped back into the bedroom.

I acted nonchalant, but I knew we had come to a defining moment in our marriage. Roger just looked at me, and I blurted out, "I don't think I can ever have a drink. Will you never have a drink with me for the rest of our lives?"

I look back at that day, when we had been wed for only twenty-four hours, and I'm still amazed at Roger's answer. Without skipping a beat, he replied, "Yes."

That was more than twenty-one years ago, and to date neither of us has had a drink. Little did I know how important it would be to have someone so close to me support me in every moment or at every party where there was alcohol—and to be willing to be the only other person to toast with water instead of wine. I will be forever grateful to God for giving me a husband who understands my weakness and has never been ashamed of me or caused me to stumble. What a friend Roger has been to me.

Exactly twenty years after our honeymoon, I decided to attend a traditional Twelve-Step meeting for the first time. I know that it sounds a bit backward to abstain from alcohol for twenty years and *then* to attend your first meeting for alcoholics. But I had consistently been a part of other support groups.

During that first Twelve-Step meeting, I became aware that sobriety anniversaries were celebrated with "chips," designating the number of days or years that a person had abstained from drugs or alcohol. When I—the first-timer—shared with the women that I was celebrating twenty years of sobriety, the room erupted with shared excitement for my accomplishment.

When I arrived home that evening, Roger asked me how the meeting went. I had to brag. "Guess what? Next week when I attend the meeting, they're going to give me a twenty-year chip. It's so rare, they didn't have one at the meeting!"

He promptly replied, "Well, when you get your chip, get me one, too."

Lord, help us to bear our mate's weaknesses. Help us to encourage and support each other, to accept each other as Christ accepted us. Give us strength to say no to things that can overpower us, and give us the courage to sacrifice when needed. Amen.

Honey, Would You . . .

Dr. Kevin Leman

It is more blessed to give than to receive.

Acts 20:35

One of the best conversations my wife, Sande, and I ever had happened a few years ago, when I decided to solicit her ideas on how I could be a better husband and a good friend. I asked her to name at least ten things she really appreciates and wants me to do regularly. Here's what she told me:

1. Whenever I'm sick, I appreciate your taking the kids to church anyway.

2. I like it when you scratch and rub my back to wake me up in the mornings—and when you bring me coffee.

3. I like it when you help with the dishes and picking up around the house, when you see what needs to be taken care of and you take care of it, and I don't have to point it out.

4. I also like it when you don't call attention to what you're doing to help. Rattling the empty coffee cups to let me know you're taking them to the sink doesn't impress me.

5. I love it when you say, "You need a weekend away. I've made arrangements for you to spend some time alone." Along with that, I want you to take care of the kids, not just dump them off at my mother's.

6. Oh, yes, I also really appreciate what you do for my mother, like providing her with transportation and helping her get things fixed around the house.

7. I like it when you take my car to be washed and serviced. Then I'm sure it's safe to drive.

8. You don't know how much I appreciate it when I'm at the end of my rope with the children and you take over just as they really get wild and start arguing with each other.

9. I like it when you make the plans for us to go out. You get the baby-sitter, you call up our friends and set a time to meet them—everything isn't left for me.

10. And finally, I love it when you're patient and understanding—especially if I've had a bad day. Like the time you came home after I drove the car through the garage door. You had to have seen the door when you drove up, but you walked in and said, "Honey, how was your day?" I said, "Oh, fine!" and I was almost ready to cry when you said, "Let's go out to dinner."

Obviously, your spouse would have a different list of things she or he appreciates having you do that express the kind of companionship, support, and love we all long for in our marriage relationships. Try exchanging your own lists soon. You'll probably learn a good deal—about needs you're meeting and about some you aren't. You'll also get ideas about how to do better. All in all, it's a great way to learn how to be the kind of pal you want to be—and to help your mate do the same for you.

Lord, sometimes we get so caught up in thinking about how our spouse can meet our needs that we forget it is more blessed to give than to receive. Help each of us to express love and companionship toward the other in ways that are meaningful. And thank you for the joy of friendship within our marriage. Amen.

CHEERS

Rachael Crabb

A man that hath friends must show himself friendly.

PROVERBS 18:24 KJV

Some days I need a person to be the Bible in shoe leather for me. I need to see Jesus in someone. Often, that "someone" is my husband.

Marriage provides us with the unique opportunity to "be" Jesus for our mate in the lowest of lows and the highest of highs in life. Larry has been a friend who has ridden the waves with me as they have crashed into the shore—and he's been there with me when the waves have peacefully lapped the sand. Husbands and wives do that for each other. They show themselves friendly.

Larry and I have learned much about being each other's friend by watching our children and their pals. When children reach those traumatic teen years, we parents pray especially hard for them to find a good friend to share the journey.

For our younger son, Ken, that prayer was answered after we moved from Florida to Indiana as he entered seventh grade. That prayer was answered in Doug Lemon. (With the names of *Crabb*

27

and *Lemon*, the boys were destined to be pals.) These boys decided early on that they would form a law firm. Then came the problem of naming the firm. This dilemma became a friendly birthday joke for many years. When Ken turned fourteen, Doug gave him a T-shirt with "Lemon and Crabb" printed on the back. For Doug's fifteenth birthday, Ken gave him a T-shirt bearing the words "Crabb and Lemon." The boys never did start a law firm— Doug is an attorney and Ken a financial planner and they live in different states—but through all the ups and downs of life, they have shown themselves friendly toward each other. Doug and Ken cheer each other on.

Are you your mate's cheerleader? We need each other! *Carpe diem*, seize the day, and be friendly to your mate—today.

Dear Jesus, thank you for making us marriage partners. Help us each to take advantage of every day to show ourselves friendly to the other, to be his or her cheerleader. We want no regrets when you call us home to be with you.

I'M JUST
FEELING
So . . . So . . .

Becky and Roger Tirabassi

Correct, rebuke and encourage—with great
patience and careful instruction.

2 TIMOTHY 4:2

I don't know anyone who loves me more or is more patient with me than my husband, Roger, who has been my spiritual mentor for all but the first three months of my Christian life. I attribute our healthy relationships with God and each other to Roger's strong convictions, honest communication, tender love, and godly ways—especially when it means correcting me. In this way he has shown himself to be a friend of the highest order, willing to tell me the truth when I can't see it.

Recently, I spent a few days struggling with a feeling I couldn't name. Whatever this feeling was, it affected my responses to everything and everyone. Because I couldn't put a label on it, I didn't know how to talk to anyone about it. But by holding it in, I couldn't experience relief or make progress in identifying the nature of my discomfort.

29

So I asked Rog if he would go for a walk to the park with the dog and me to give me some quick counsel before I left for a speaking engagement. As soon as we walked down the porch steps, I said, "Okay, I need a little counsel. I've been struggling with something and can't seem to get past the emotions I'm feeling." Then I told him about my fears and feelings.

Roger, like the good friend he is, always gently corrects me, but this time, after only a few minutes together, he was more direct. "Becky, what you are talking about is covetousness, which is one of the Ten Commandments [see Exodus 20:17]. The emotion you're using lots of words to describe is really plain old jealousy. Perhaps the reason you're emotionally unsettled is because you're struggling with *sin* rather than an emotion."

Oddly, I wasn't hurt by his honesty. I immediately sensed a measure of relief that he had identified the reason for my discomfort. I also knew what I had to do next to be free . . . As soon as I was seated on the airplane, I turned to the "Admit" section of my prayer notebook and in writing confessed to God my sin of jealousy.

At my speaking engagement the following day, I shared my struggle with the sin of covetousness and how Roger had corrected, rebuked, and encouraged me on our walk around the block. When everyone laughed at my confusing emotions and sin, I realized we all struggle with our emotions. But until we identify and turn from the sin *behind* those emotions, we won't experience complete healing in our lives and relationships. I thank my friend and my husband for helping me to move on from vague feelings into a wonderfully good feeling—peace with God.

Be good mates to one another; help each other to identify what sometimes lies behind the smokescreen of your feelings and to see more clearly why you feel as you do, and what to do about it. But above all, remember to do it as a friend—gently and "with great patience and careful instruction," as the verse for today suggests.

> *Lord, help us each to be the kind of spouse who is encouraging and affirming of our partner. And when necessary, please give us the honesty and safety within our relationship to gently help the other to see a blind spot and to receive words of correction. Give us great patience, compassion, and a genuine willingness to forgive each other every day—and in a loving way.*

Part Two
Celebrating Our Imperfections

THE FINE ART OF STUBBORNNESS

Neil Clark Warren

*Then he said to Thomas, "Put your finger here; see
my hands. Reach out your hand and put it into my side.
Stop doubting and believe." Thomas said to
him, "My Lord and my God!"*

JOHN 20:27–28

Stubbornness can be understood two ways. On the one hand,
if you're "unreasonably or perversely unyielding," you may
be that kind of stubborn we think of as "mulish." But if you are
"justifiably unyielding," you may be the kind of stubborn we sort
of admire—"resolute."

Marylyn and I sometimes are stubborn in our marriage. I am,
of course, usually quite resolute, but the word that comes to my
mind about her stubbornness is, indeed, the word "mulish." She
might stubbornly refuse to accept my perspective here, but that
word "mulish" pops into my mind again. When I stubbornly hold
out for more conditions to be met before I adjust my attitude on
something, it's because of my sterling character, my resoluteness,

to be exact. For some reason, her stubbornness seems less high and holy. Yes, in fact, sort of mulish.

Let me give you an example of Marylyn's mulishness. She wants to add two rooms to our house, and she wants to add an eating area to the kitchen. Now, I ask you, does that make any sense? It strikes me as expensive, disruptive to our daily functioning, and far from the best use of our resources. She has all kinds of silly reasons to justify her wishes, but I, of course, in my resolute way, hold out for rationality and good sense.

Marylyn thinks I'm being stubborn about this remodeling job, that I'm refusing to recognize the wisdom of her position. She's the one, of course, who's being stubborn! If I resolutely refuse to join her folly, maybe she'll see the light. My resoluteness will save us thousands of dollars.

Another stubborn man, whom I hope I don't take after, is Thomas in the Scripture for today. He wasn't with the other disciples on that Sunday evening when Jesus "suddenly . . . was standing there among them" (John 20:19 LB). On that occasion, Jesus showed the disciples his hands and side, and they, of course, were convinced this person was their risen Lord. When they saw Thomas later, they told him of their experience with Jesus, but Thomas said, "Unless I see the nail marks in his hands and put my finger where the nails were, and put my hand into his side, I will not believe it" (John 20:25).

Now, here's my question to you: Was Thomas unreasonably and perversely unyielding, sort of mulish? Or was he justifiably unyielding, resolute? Did his stubbornness contribute to the things that really mattered, or did it get in the way, slow things down, create frustration for everyone else?

Stubbornness in marriage can be horribly frustrating for a marriage partner and punishing to a whole family. When a person's stubborn attitude keeps getting in the way of reasonable progress, the only word to describe it is "mulish."

But sometimes one person's willingness to stand against ideas and behavior that would lead to marital and family harm is the only thing that saves a marriage or a family from devastating pain. It takes courage to stand against the popular will of the group or of a strong partner. Others may call this stubbornness, but I call it character—resoluteness.

Okay, I confess: I haven't been resolute too often in my life; I'm much more often mulish. But I'm proud of myself for one set of events in our family history. Our oldest daughter, Lorrie, now a great mother of four boys, often wanted to see R-rated movies when she was in her mid-teens. I stubbornly refused to let her do this, and she was convinced I was mulish to the core. We had many a go-round in our kitchen. She argued that "all the other parents are letting their kids go." It didn't matter to me. I knew it wasn't good for her, and I held out. Now, she's glad I did, and she's ready to protect her boys in the same way.

In the case of the apostle Thomas, Jesus willingly dealt with the disciple's stubborn demands. Jesus encouraged Thomas to put his finger into the nail prints, and to put his hand into Jesus' wounded side. And Thomas's stubbornness eventually led to one of the most dramatic moments in biblical history—when he proclaimed, "My Lord and my God!"

How about the stubbornness in your marriage? Does it represent a marriage-sabotaging meanness, or is it sometimes an indication of deep-down character strength that saves your marriage from pain and torment?

Mulishness can keep your marriage from soaring, but resoluteness can provide a core marital strength. Somehow, both partners need to rid themselves of the former and reinforce and celebrate the latter.

Dear Lord Jesus, we don't want to be destructively stubborn. Help us to get over that. But we do want to be strong and resolute. Give us an eye and a heart for that kind of strength. In the middle of our marriage, will you make us soft toward each other, eager to please one another, but will you help us to be like steel when we need to be for your sake? Amen.

ALL
WASHED
UP

Becky and Roger Tirabassi

But the fruit of the Spirit is love, joy, peace, patience,
kindness, goodness, faithfulness, gentleness and self-control.

GALATIANS 5:22

When Roger and I were first married, I did most of the home chores, including the laundry. Unfortunately, I had a knack for shrinking clothes—anyone's and everyone's. Many of the men's one hundred percent cotton sweatshirts I washed became mine—after only one washing. Eventually, Roger took over the laundry duties, not only because I traveled a few days in each week but also because, when he did that chore, his clothes came out of the dryer the same size as when they entered the washer.

But recently, we experienced a Roger-sponsored laundry disaster. I purchased a pair of black jeans that were one hundred percent cotton. I didn't want them to shrink in the waist or in length because my local store didn't have these jeans in my size, and this pair had been mailed to me from out-of-state. I hadn't even worn the jeans yet.

I picked a day to wash them when no one was home and no other laundry needed to be done. I filled the washing machine with cold water and poured in a small amount of liquid soap, being careful not to let the soap touch the jeans. Then I set the rinse cycle for "delicate."

The washing machine was swishing away when I decided to run an errand, knowing that, when I returned home, I would hang the jeans to dry.

An hour later I sashayed into the house to hear the dryer thrumming away. I felt a cold sweat break out on my forehead. I dropped my keys and bag and dashed from the front door, through the family room, and into the laundry room. That's when I almost ran down Roger. The only words that came out of my mouth were, "You didn't . . ."

With a shocked look but without another word, we both ran into the laundry room. I got there first and whipped open the door to the dryer to find a single pair of black jeans rolling over and over. I quickly pulled them out and felt how hot they were. They had to have been drying for an hour!

Roger looked ready to defend himself against whatever comment I was going to fling toward him. I could just envision his reasoning: More times than either of us could count, I had shrunk the entire family's clothes; Roger often and willingly did the laundry; how was he supposed to know that tossing these jeans into the dryer would constitute his biggest laundry error . . .

I knew that I had to make a decision. On the one hand, if I wanted to fight about this, we were going to have a doozy that would include all twenty-one years of each other's laundry faux pas. On the other hand, the previous Sunday our pastor had given a message about the powerful effect the Holy Spirit should have on a believer's life. The theme verse was Galatians 5:22,

"But the fruit of the Spirit is love, joy, peace, patience, kindness, goodness, faithfulness and self-control."

During the sermon, I had asked myself, *Do I live, especially in my own home, as if I'm filled with the Holy Spirit?* Now it appeared as if I was going to get my chance!

But before I could even say, "What were you thinking?" Roger began a monologue of why he thought he was helping me out by drying my jeans. He also wondered aloud why no note was on top of the dryer, warning him not to put the jeans in.

When he paused to launch into his next argument, I said, "It's okay."

Both of us were taken aback by my response, which washed up the long list of arguments we had ready to lash out at each other. A profound Bible verse that had been . . .

read at church,

illustrated in a few examples by the pastor,

written down in my notes during the service, and

meditated on during my quiet time that afternoon

. . . gave me the power I needed to live above my circumstances and to be guided by the Holy Spirit to respond in a way that was out of character for me.

And you know what? That same principle holds true when we encounter imperfections in one another. The Holy Spirit waits for us to pause, make a choice, and respond "in character"—or rather, in *his* character instead of our own.

Father in heaven, thanks for the Bible. In it, we find the way to live our lives with patience and gentleness. Forgive us for taking matters into our own hands. Fill us with your Holy Spirit that we might display the joy, peace, patience, kindness, goodness, faithfulness, gentleness, and self-control that will allow us to experience a great marriage.

The Milkshake, the Briefcase, and the Carpet

Les and Leslie Parrott

Love is patient.

1 Corinthians 13:4

I (Les) had just finished a marathon day of teaching back-to-back courses as well as guest lecturing for a colleague at the university. My body was weary, and my mind was even more fatigued.

On my commute home, I decided to stop by a new snack shop near the campus that, according to my students, made terrific milkshakes. I thought a thick chocolate number might energize my body and mind—you know, make me a better husband for the evening. And Leslie wouldn't need to know about it since I'd be getting home in time to sit down for that hot meal she would have ready. *So I don't eat as much lemon chicken and rice tonight,* I rationalized.

But when I walked into the shop, I realized this was not going to be an ordinary milkshake. They called it a Chocolate Colossus, and it was made with soymilk, sorbet, and other healthful ingredients.

Yuk! I muttered under my breath.

"What kind of power boost do you want in it?" the teenage clerk asked. He was wearing more earrings in a single ear than anyone I'd seen outside the pages of *National Geographic*.

"Excuse me?" I said sheepishly, as if I were from a foreign country or maybe another planet and didn't understand the customs underlying his question.

"You get a free boost with the Colossus," the kid said, as he pointed to the handmade sign behind him.

After he added an "energizing" powder to my drink, I was on my way. I took one sip through a skinny straw and realized this was not the treat I had in mind. *Oh, well,* I thought, *it won't spoil my dinner.* I set the drink inside the zippered opening of my soft leather briefcase to keep the shake from spilling while I drove.

By the time I pulled into the garage I had forgotten all about the shake. I walked into the house, set my bag in the living room, and headed straight up the stairs to squeeze my wife hello.

Should I mention at this point that just one week earlier my wife had had the carpets professionally cleaned?

You know the feeling, don't you? That "oh no" that erupts from deep inside in response to a simple little question like, "Honey, what's that oozing out of your briefcase onto the newly cleaned carpet?" That hesitancy to turn and look. That sinking feeling of discovering a chocolate soy sauce trail forging its way into the newly cleaned fibers. We have all been there, face to face with our own blunders and poised to accept the wrath we have earned.

But do you also know the relief at such a moment of hearing your spouse's laughter, rather than anger? I do, and I am very grateful.

One of the most loving presents we can give our partner is the gift of patience. Perhaps that's why Paul begins his litany of love in 1 Corinthians 13 with that particular quality. When we cultivate patience, we can endure frustrations and inconvenience without going crazy. After all, that's what patience is all about—tolerating frustration.

And that's exactly the present Leslie gave me the day I came home with a milkshake in my briefcase. Though I know she was miffed about the mess, she didn't let that stand in her way. She even managed to find humor in the situation.

Love is patient, and that's good because spouses are imperfect. And just as our patience is almost exhausted, love empowers us to find a little more. So "power up" with an extra dollop of patience the next time your spouse shows just how imperfect he or she is.

> *Father, give us the patience to respond with love when our partner does something frustrating. Give us a perspective to see the big picture and to remember that neither of us is perfect. Thank you for your patience and grace as we each work to be the person you want us to be.*

THE BAGEL SHOP

Nicole Johnson

[Love] keeps no record of wrongs.

1 CORINTHIANS 13:5

We stood with the pastor at the door of the church where we had just performed, and shook parishoners' hands. The morning had been wonderful. The worship service was powerful, and we had brought a message on God's unconditional grace and acceptance through our major drama sketch called "The Ledger People." In it, a couple keeps score on everything: their kids, their friends, and, of course, each other. We spoke after the drama about laying down our ledgers and receiving God's love as a free gift, not earning it, not deserving it, not trying to pay it back, just receiving it—gracefully and graciously. Score-keeping flies directly in the gospel's face. But we do it every day.

We packed up our props and headed to a nearby bagel shop to grab a bite of lunch before we returned to our hotel. We ended up chatting with a couple from the church while we stood in line. The bagel shop was a casual place, and we conversed about grace as we stared up at the chalkboard menu behind the counter.

Finally, I decided on a vegetable bagel with salmon spread, and Paul ordered a pizza bagel with extra cheese. We worked our way to the cash register and were laughing with this couple, when the cashier responded to Paul's outstretched credit card by saying, "Sir, we only accept cash."

Our laughter stopped. Paul returned the card to his wallet and looked at me with panic. "Do you have any cash?" he whispered.

"No," I confessed, starting to feel embarrassed. "Will you take a check?" I asked.

"I'm sorry," the young cashier replied. "We only accept cash."

We all stood there for an uncomfortable moment. Then the couple behind us offered to buy our lunch.

I felt mortified. Why should they buy our lunch? Because we didn't read the sign? "Oh, no," I protested. Surely we could find another option, figure something else out. No checks, hmmm. What about a nearby ATM? The longer we stood there, the more uncomfortable everyone became.

"We would love to buy your lunch," the woman said. "We were so blessed by you this morning, and this is a way for us to say thank you."

I felt my heart stiffen and my mental pencil sharpen. My ledger was screaming so I said, "Well, we'll pay you back this evening when we get some cash."

I saw their faces fall. "You don't have to pay us back," the man assured.

Paul suggested, "How about a free video?"

I thought, *How about we practice what we preach? Dear Jesus, forgive me.* After performing a rousing rendition of "The Ledger People," right there in the bagel shop, I wanted to pay back the money,

I wanted to even the score, I wanted to do anything to keep from looking needy or poor.

Humbling your heart to receive when you're in need is far more difficult than giving. Givers are in control. Receivers are out of control and helpless. I would rather be anything but out of control and helpless. Self-sufficiency is king in our culture, and it was king of my heart that morning.

But love doesn't keep score. It can't. When we're trying to love, we can't be trying to win, to look good, to protect our reputation, or to balance the ledger. When couples keep score, both of them lose. If our relationships become more about who has taken out the trash how many times versus who put the kids to bed how many nights in a row, our love will not survive. One of Webster's definitions of love is "a score of zero, as in the game of tennis." Love is never going to even up, balance out, or be equally fair. But it will be humbling, life-changing, and deeply satisfying, if we can throw away the score cards and close the ledgers.

Every day presents a bagel shop of its own. When we're confronted with the free gift of the gospel, will we receive it, or will we try to pay our own way? Will we say that we believe God's love is unconditional yet all the while try to earn it? When the cashiers in our lives humble us with the cash-only rules, and we don't have it, can we look toward heaven or others in our lives, spouses included, and allow them to love us? It is more blessed to give than to receive because receiving is harder!

We let the couple in line behind us buy our lunch. All afternoon we pondered God's gift and our reluctance to receive it, even though we had preached on it that morning. We came away with new astonishment about the God of heaven who paid our way into the richest life imaginable when we didn't have the cash—thoughts that we would have missed if we had bought our own bagels.

Father, keep confronting us with the truth of the gospel. We don't like needing you. We don't like needing anything, including the need to be rescued. Keep putting us in situations where we must receive grace or go hungry. Our hearts fly to independence in milliseconds, and we begin to think that we can live out your truth on our own. Thanks for buying our bagels and so much more. Amen.

HOME
IMPROVEMENT

Gary Smalley

Why do you look at the speck of sawdust in your brother's
eye and pay no attention to the plank in your own eye?

MATTHEW 7:3

A church council meeting's agenda can be a real snoozer. The routine reports, budget reviews, and voting usually send everyone home yawning. But then there was the council meeting in which, as a youth pastor who had been out of seminary for two years, I delivered my report enthusiastically, hoping to add some excitement to the typically boring meeting. The excitement I generated wasn't the kind I expected. But I did learn an important principle that enabled me to draw closer to Christ, to the people who hurt me, and to my wife.

My report consisted mostly of recommendations for what I considered obvious needs, particularly the purchase of a church bus for the youth. But instead of endorsing my recommendations and expressing what a wonderful job I was doing, each council member started to criticize me. Why didn't I run the youth group as it had been run in previous years? I should slow down in making so many changes. Did I think my ways were superior?

The intense criticism stunned me, and I was offended that no one supported me, not even the pastor. I slithered home and woke Norma to pour out my woes. I complained about how I'd been mistreated and mentioned that I ought to quit. She tried to encourage me, but nothing she said seemed to help.

Finally, unable to sleep, I sat in the kitchen and pondered my situation. On the scratch pad by the phone I wrote, "Why do people in the church continue to hurt my feelings? Why do they make me so angry?"

"Lord," I pleaded, "show me what I can do to expose the hardness of these people's hearts. What would it take to break through their stubborn resistance and help them see your love?" If necessary, I was willing to stay up all night and read every chapter of the Bible to find out how to solve the problem.

It never occurred to me that the conflict with the church might be my fault, that I might need to adjust some of my attitudes and actions. I could only think that if "those people" were more supportive, more committed to Christ, more dedicated, I'd be happy. If they would only step out of the past and start implementing my fresh ideas, I wouldn't have these problems.

Sound familiar? No wonder in Matthew 7:3 Jesus felt the need to tell us that the problem might not be the speck in someone else's eye.

One of the biggest questions I ask a couple in crisis is "What will it take to make this relationship better?" If either or both of them answer, "Well, if he (she) would just change, then this relationship would improve," then I tell them their situation won't improve until they realize that they can only work on themselves. The power to change is only held by ourselves and God. We can't control the beliefs and actions of others.

So the next time you find yourself up late at night, scratching thoughts on a pad of paper about how your mate needs to change, remember me at the church council meeting. I finally figured out the problem was a lot more about me and a lot less about "them" than I had initially thought. May you figure that out faster than I did.

Lord, help each of us to uncover our eyes to the things about ourselves we don't wish to see, uncover our ears to the things we don't wish to hear, and uncover our hearts to the things we don't want to know. Amen.

When "I Don't Care" Means Something Else

Dr. Kevin Leman

> *Do nothing from selfishness or empty conceit,*
> *but with humility of mind let each of you regard*
> *one another as more important than himself.*
>
> PHILIPPIANS 2:3 NASB

A husband can show affection to his wife in many ways, if he really knows the person he is married to. To a woman, affection is having her husband know what she likes and be willing to go out of his way to say in different ways, "I love you, I care about you."

Some husbands don't have a clue about how to do this, and they often excuse themselves by saying, "She knows I'm not the affectionate type." Others at least try to do the affectionate thing, but they blow it because they don't work hard enough at knowing their wives and what they really want.

Picture the following scene: It's Friday night, and the wife has arrived at home from work before her husband. She's just starting to think about preparing dinner when her husband drags in after his week of fighting deadlines and freeways. This is the man who used to leave her love notes under the windshield wipers when they were in college. Or who slipped love notes under her apartment door when they were dating. This is the same handsome lover who walked her down the aisle and before God and man said, "I do." Now, after several years of marriage, he comes home on Friday night and mutters such romantic nothings as "Is there any mail?" and "What's for dinner?"

Questions like these make the typical wife want to soar—as in "hit the ceiling." Just then, however, the perceptive hubby notes that something is missing. "By the way, where are the kids?"

"The kids? They're all at Grandma's to stay overnight—it's just the two of us for dinner."

"Just the *two* of us?" The weary knight of the freeways is starting to come to.

"Yes," replies his wife.

"Put that stuff away—forget about making anything. I'll take you out to dinner."

His wife needs to hear those magic words, "out to dinner," only once. She's in the car in a flash. Her husband joins her a few seconds later because he *walked* to the car. (Sometimes I think the three little words every woman loves to hear aren't "I love you" but "out to dinner.")

The husband and wife are driving into town, and he turns to her and says, "Honey, where would you like to go to dinner?"

What does she say? As only wives can, she responds, "Oh, I don't care."

Using his naturally keen insight, our perceptive hero concludes, "Well, she doesn't seem to care where we go." His male mind continues to function with computerlike speed as he reasons, *I'm dead tired anyway, and the kids aren't home so maybe we'll just get a quick bite to eat, and then . . .*

"Honey," he says as he turns back to her with what he thinks is an adoring look, "what do you say we go down and see the colonel?"

Her mouth agape, his wife stares back at him. "The colonel? As in Kentucky Fried Chicken? *You want to take me to see the colonel?*"

A deep freeze instantaneously fills the car. This husband had better like his chicken cold because that's the way things will be for the rest of the evening. You see, this husband missed the point. When his wife responded to his question, she didn't exactly mean, "I don't care." Of course she cared. Furthermore, she thought to herself, *If he really loves me, he'll instinctively know where I want to go for dinner.*

Now, who's at fault here? We have to say the husband was on the right track to suggest dinner out. But we have to reach the verdict of "guilty as charged" for not realizing dinner out to his wife means "make it something special." She wanted him to know her well enough to suggest a cozy locale. Candlelight would have earned him bonus points. Holding her hand during the meal would have sent her soaring—to cloud nine. Ultimately, she wanted him to communicate, "I know you, I know you intimately, and I want to meet your needs. I want to make you happy." Come on guys, you can do it!

Of course, we have to convict the wife of a common crime: expecting her husband to read her mind. We guys need some help here, ladies. At least throw us a few hints so we can sniff out the right choice. Say something like, "Oh, a quiet place where we can sit and talk would be nice." That leaves plenty of room for choices, but pretty much eliminates fast food spots and joints with big screen TVs blaring out some sporting event.

Okay, so we're all imperfect and need a little help to get it right. Men, keep in mind that "I don't care" doesn't mean "I don't care" but "Show me you care." Got it, guys? And for the women, a few parameters to keep us guys from bumbling around would be much appreciated, thank you very much.

> *Father, help us to be alert enough to make choices that please our partner. And give us the insight to study our spouse so we know what is pleasing to him or her. But above all, Lord, bless us with forgiving spirits when we mess up what could be moments of special closeness. Amen.*

I Said, "Rest— or Else!"

Neil Clark Warren

For in six days the Lord made heaven and earth, and rested on the seventh day, and was refreshed.

EXODUS 31:17 LB

I'm not much of a rester, and neither is my wife, Marylyn. We're far more comfortable working than we are resting. And, if you can imagine it, I actually *like* to wear a long-sleeved white shirt with a tie. I'm fairly confident I'm better-looking that way. And I like Marylyn much better in high heels—the kind she wears when she's working. So, if you need a couple on your team who can go till they drop, give us a call. You'll have to leave a message, of course, because we'll probably be out working.

I do get tired once in a while, but I really don't have time to take a nap. My friend Steve Sohlberg says, "I can rest when I die," and I think he might have the right approach. When you're sleeping, you don't move closer to any goals, you can't check anything off your "to do" list, and you sure can't feel good about yourself. I came to the conclusion a long time ago that the primary motivation that drives us all is to feel good about ourselves.

But whoever heard of a person getting up from a nap with a stronger sense of inner worth, a healthier degree of self-esteem? I usually get up with a groggy feeling, sometimes with a headache. I don't think resting is for me.

I must admit I've read studies to the effect that anger mismanagement usually occurs under the influence of alcohol or fatigue. Since I get a headache when I drink anything alcoholic, I don't have to worry about yelling at somebody when I'm inebriated. But I must say that I'm kind of cranky when I'm really tired.

Marylyn and I have been traveling around the United States doing marriage seminars almost every weekend, and Marylyn and my colleagues have been hurting my feelings pretty frequently lately. But it couldn't be my fatigue, could it?

My buddy Kevin Leman, who is, I think, the funniest speaker in America, called me "the old grouch" when he and I were in a meeting in Dallas a couple of months ago. And after that meeting, Steve Arterburn, the genius behind our Couples of Faith team, was overheard saying, "Neil will be all right as soon as he gets a good night's rest." Maybe there *is* something to this "rest" business.

I notice that I love bragging about how much I do. Of course, I do it in the name of complaining about how overworked I am. What's that all about? By the way, did you know I'm the hardest working psychologist in America? It's terrible the pace I have to keep. I have a full practice of twenty-five or thirty clients every week, I speak everywhere, and I . . . but maybe you're tired of this. Maybe you'd just like to tell me to go take a nap. Maybe you think I could do more for the human race if I'd allocate some of my schedule to resting. At the very least, you think, I wouldn't be such an insufferable grouch.

The text from Exodus 31 speaks clearly enough about the importance of rest. When God was talking to Moses, the Lord didn't leave any room for misunderstanding. In fact, he sort of pounded his fist on the table. "Yes, rest on the Sabbath, for it is holy. Anyone who does not obey this command must die; anyone who does any work on that day shall be killed" (verses 14–15 LB).

I'd better look at this matter of rest a little more carefully. This is getting serious.

The Lord makes it clear why we should rest on the Sabbath day: "It helps you to remember that I am Jehovah who makes you holy" (verse 13 LB). Oh, now I'm beginning to see! If I've been working my head off to make myself a more likely recipient of God's love and favor, I'm investing my hope in the wrong place. *He* makes me "holy," and try as hard as I might, *I* never can. He is God, and I am the creature; I have to start remembering that.

Okay, I'm going to start resting more. If it makes me a better marriage partner, a happier colleague, a "holier" person, I'm going to try to fit it into my schedule. How about you?

> *Lord Jesus, we work too much and rest too little. Somehow we keep forgetting about the need to rest. Please help us to stay alert to this crucial principle. And the next time one of us takes a nap, help us to remember that you are Jehovah who makes us holy. We need your help. Amen.*

THE
TEN
LEPERS

Nicole Johnson

*One of them, when he saw he was healed, came back,
praising God in a loud voice. He threw himself at Jesus'
feet and thanked him. . . . Jesus asked, "Were not all
ten cleansed? Where are the other nine?"*

LUKE 17:15–17

High in the Colorado Rockies, a group of about two hundred gathered for a special celebration, the anniversary of a counseling retreat center that, for twenty-five years, had helped couples over marital stumbling blocks. Paul and I had gone to this retreat center six or seven years before, and the experience had enhanced our marriage. So now we returned to celebrate with the staff and friends.

When we arrived, I asked the leader, "How many alumni couples are coming for the weekend?"

"Four," was his reply.

I was puzzled. All through the celebration I wondered why so few couples had come. Did the majority of them end up divorcing? Maybe we were among the few who had worked through some issues and stayed married.

"Actually, our success rate is quite high," the leader told me when I asked him. "But, Nicole, many people who come here view the retreat as one of the dark times in their marriage. They don't want to identify with that again or celebrate it."

I continued to think about that. And I heard Jesus' haunting question after he had healed ten lepers and only one came back to say thanks. "Were not all ten cleansed? Where are the other nine?" I thought about those couples who had found healing at this retreat center. Weren't there hundreds?

Then it was as if a light came on. Those lepers identified Jesus with their leprosy rather than with their healing. When they thought of Jesus, they remembered the sores, the wounds, and the pain rather than the joy, the freedom, and the life.

That's why many of the couples were still at home. That's why, when their invitations arrived in the mail, dark feelings rose up, maybe even shame and embarrassment. When those couples thought about the retreat, they thought about the pain and anguish they were in at the time rather than the healing that had begun to take place there.

How often do we reject what started our healing because we don't want to revisit the dark? We're embarrassed about our pain or that we went through deep struggles. We identify Christ with the anguish, and never see the good he brought out of the process.

Because the couples didn't return, they missed the celebration. They missed the opportunity to see with newly opened eyes this Savior who had rescued them. And they aren't the only ones. People who never call doctors to thank them after their lives have been saved. Men and women who were rescued from drowning or from a serious accident who never respond to their rescuers. They want to forget and move on. "I'm better now. I'm saved; I'm whole; I'm clean. Why would I want to revisit that time?"

Because, dear friends, life is celebration. Life is thanksgiving. Life is gratitude. And because we don't find joy without pain. We don't give thanks without tribulation. We can't erase pieces of our history—namely the dark, painful parts—and expect to have a glorious future. The hard parts are what make the glory. We don't begin on this journey once we "get better." Every piece of life is part of the journey that brought us to this place, and to miss that is to miss God's plan and purpose. There is no healing without wounds, no freedom without chains, and no life without death.

Have you connected someone's help in your life with the pain or with the healing? Is there someone—perhaps your spouse—whom you have been reluctant to thank or praise? Have you struggled with your faith in Christ because you have attached his presence to dark days that you never want to relive? Consider integrating the joy and the anguish as part of a life well lived. Return to your place of suffering and thank the healing hand that brought you through.

Jesus, forgive us for not returning to thank you more. Give us grace for those times when we have gotten on with our lives without returning to you, because looking back caused too much embarrassment or shame. And Jesus, thank you for releasing us from our chains, for healing our wounds, and for cleansing us from our spiritual leprosy. We are returning now to say thank you. Amen.

THE ULTIMATE LOVE LESSON

Les and Leslie Parrott

Who shall separate us from the love of Christ? Shall trouble or hardship or persecution or famine or nakedness or danger or sword? . . . No, in all these things we are more than conquerors through him who loved us.

ROMANS 8:35, 37

In his Oscar-winning role in *Good Will Hunting*, Robin Williams provides a unique spin on love and intimacy. He tells a young, less-experienced man that loving someone is about accepting the quirks, the peculiar habits that only lovers can share. This sharing of the authentic self—one not entirely apparent to anyone else in the world—is what relationships are built on and fortified by. Some of the habits might be cute or humorous; other idiosyncrasies are decidedly serious. The point is that, if you love someone, you accept who he or she really is.

That's a tough lesson for most couples to learn. Let's be honest. It's so much easier to love who we want our spouses to be—not who they really are. I know you feel that way. We all do. It's one of the most pervasive therapeutic issues we see in counseling couples. Almost every couple who comes to our door is frustrated that the other person in the partnership isn't feeling, thinking, or being the kind of person the other individual desires. Who wouldn't find it a breeze to love a partner who did all the things we wanted? Instead, we're called as couples to love our partners when they are irritatingly, even maddeningly, insensitive, lazy, quirky, or downright selfish. We aren't called to love them as their ideal selves, but as their authentic selves. The question is how.

We don't know what the psychologist in *Good Will Hunting* would say, but we can tell you what we believe and what we know from experience. The answer is found in our relationship with God and his love for us. He gives us the ultimate love lesson.

Think of it this way: How you perceive God's love shapes your love for each other. God's love is self-sacrificing (John 15:13), unchangeable (Psalm 33:11), and compelling (2 Corinthians 5:14). God's love is also jealous (Exodus 20:5; 34:14; Deuteronomy 4:24; 5:9; 6:15). This may sound strange to modern ears, but a beautiful concept lies behind this kind of "jealous" love. To say that God is a jealous God is to say that God is the lover of men and women and that his heart can have no rival. He must have the whole devotion of our hearts. The divine-human relationship is not that of king and subject, nor that of master and servant, nor that of owner and slave, nor that of judge and defendant, but that of lover and loved one, a relationship that only can be paralleled in the perfect marriage relationship between husband and wife.

"When I stop to think," writes Ruth Bell Graham, "of all that love should be—accepting, forgiving, supporting, strengthening—God is all that and more. He is perfect love." And when Ruth Graham feels that her love for her husband, Billy, doesn't measure up to such divine standards, she says, "At that moment

Romans 8:31–39 comes into my consciousness, and I am surrounded again by an awareness of God's love. He loves me in spite of me!"

Have you ever felt as if your love wasn't all you wanted it to be? You're not alone. Only God's love is perfect. So in your journey to become soulmates, pray that you will be "filled to the measure of all the fullness of God" (Ephesians 3:19). It's the only way we know to love someone as he or she really is.

> *Gracious God, lover of our souls, we ask you to reveal your love to us as a couple. Show us your love for us as individuals through our partner's loving actions. And teach us to love as you do. We aspire to live a life that reflects your love, allowing you to transform our marriage into one of rare character. Thank you for a love from which nothing can separate us. Amen.*

Part Three
Celebrating Family and Home

GRAVEYARD ROOTS

Dr. Kevin Leman

God sets the lonely in families.

PSALM 68:6

I believe it's so important that children connect with their extended families that I dream up special field trips for that purpose. One summer day a number of years back—when our girls were just starting into their teens, Kevie was still a little guy, and Hannah didn't exist yet—I bundled the whole family into the car and headed over to a little town called Gowanda, about thirty miles south of Buffalo. My destination was a cemetery, but I didn't let everyone know that at first.

As we drove along, I pointed out various landmarks: "That's where Daddy used to fish . . . That's where Daddy played his first Little League game."

I fully expected my kids to be all eyes and ears. Instead, I glanced in the rearview mirror and saw one of my teenage daughters with her eyes closed in obvious bliss. She was all ears, all right—bobbing her head back and forth to whatever was coming in over the headphones connected to her Walkman.

Undaunted, I drove on to the cemetery just outside Gowanda. As we pulled up to the gate and my kids realized that this was where I was taking them, there were cries of dismay. Dad had really lost it—probably eating too much oat bran again.

But I didn't mind. I knew my kids had never been to a cemetery, much less the cemetery that held the Leman family plot. When I told them there was a headstone in that cemetery with our family's name on it, they perked up.

"You mean, it actually says *Leman?*" Krissy asked.

"Yep," I replied sagely.

"All right!" they all chorused, and then they were off, looking as intently as if they hoped to find gold. At least twenty minutes later I heard cries of "We found it, we found it." Sure enough, there was the Leman headstone, surrounded by many other smaller markers in the family plot. We wound up taking pictures with the kids draped all over "our" headstone.

I won't forget that day. Like my wife and children, I had never visited this cemetery before. I had an eerie feeling as we looked at the Leman headstone and all those other grave markers. They were mute testimony to how quickly life passes. There was Uncle Val, Great-Aunt Fannie, and my great-grandfather, John Henry Leman. Oh, yes, and there, in a corner of the plot, was my grandfather's marker—Joseph Leman, who froze to death one night after collapsing dead drunk in a snowbank. All of them had been real people, living out their lives with their own families, and now they were gone.

I tell you this story not to indulge my own nostalgia but to remind you that your family's roots are important, too. So many families I know are missing out on this. Do you think Alex Haley's book and the miniseries were successful simply on the strength of Haley's writing? Of course not. Haley is a fine writer, but in *Roots* he struck a chord that goes much deeper than that. What *Roots* said to millions was: "If you don't know where you came from, you'll never get to where you want to go."

I'm afraid that too many families have sacrificed something very valuable and precious in the name of chasing the great American dream by pulling up stakes and heading across the country to a can't-miss business opportunity or a long-worked-for vice presidency in the corporation. I know economics are a very real part of life, but I still wonder if we aren't sacrificing some basic things on the altar of having it all, or at least having a piece of the pie.

In fact, I challenge couples not to accept the promotion at work if it means relocating the family away from family members. The extended family, for many of us, is a rich soil in which our "roots" will flourish.

How about your family? Is that move across the country worth it? What can you do to stay in touch with your relatives? How can you instill in your kids a sense of heritage? Regardless of their age, it's never too late—or too early—to start.

Father, thank you for giving us the heritage of our families. Help us to value our "inheritance," with all its good and bad qualities. And thank you that we, as a couple, have become a part of each other's family through marriage. Remind each of us to be supportive and even insistent with the other to maintain those familial ties. Help us to find time to stay in touch with family members, not taking them for granted but showing love and kindness to them—especially the cantankerous ones. Give us creative ways to communicate to our children the sense of being part of a larger whole.

THE HARDEST
WORK IN
THE WORLD

Neil Clark Warren

> *Honor your father and your mother, so that you*
> *may live long in the land the LORD your God is giving you.*
>
> EXODUS 20:12

Since my mother and father died a few years ago, I'm spending a lot more time these days quoting this verse to anyone who will listen—especially to our three daughters and to our nine grandchildren. It's about time these children come to know that their treatment of me is right at the center of the Ten Commandments. The commandment to honor me comes *before* "you shall not murder," and also before commands against lying, stealing, and committing adultery. "This business of treating your mother and father with honor is really *serious*," I stress to them. Goodness knows we deserve *some* honor for what we put up with when we were raising them! (And the same goes for us honoring our parents who somehow managed to raise *us*.)

Our three daughters were quite young when I felt the most keenly my parental helplessness. We had made a nostalgic return to Princeton, New Jersey, a town that had meant so much to us when we were in graduate school there. One of our fondest memories was eating at the Nassau Inn, a wonderful, formal old place that had fabulous food. We forgot it was a place for stodgy old fogies who wanted nothing to do with children until they were in their early forties. We were ushered to a table for five, complete with a fancy white tablecloth that reached to the floor and a lineup of forks not to be believed. Lindsay, our youngest, soon began to cry, and all eyes in the room were locked on us. We offered her every last thing in Marylyn's purse and in my pockets, but she was negotiating for a lot more—maybe our combined inheritances, we thought. With a red face, Marylyn picked Lindsay up and headed for the ladies' room.

Meanwhile, Luann, our middle child, dropped her knife on the floor and was heading after it. I thought I had her stopped when Lorrie reached for a big glass of ice water. To avert catastrophe, I dove to intervene. Because I'd taken my eyes off Luann, she continued after the knife. Having saved the water, I looked around, and Luann had disappeared. Eventually, I found her under the table where her lost knife had led to a lot of other valuable treasures. I asked her to "come up from there," but she was too curious, too focused, and too *disobedient!*

I was losing it! Lorrie went after the water again. The whole roomful of critics was outraged with me. I could still hear Lindsay crying in the restroom.

What is it about kids that makes them worth all this?

Everybody knows that children require backbreaking work from the moment they push their little heads out of the birth canal and say hello to this big world. They have to be picked up when they cry, carried everywhere, fed and bathed regularly, worried about, listened to when they fuss, taken to every kind of doctor, taught everything they know, and prayed for without ceasing.

Children have to be loved unconditionally, trusted to "look both ways," treated with patience and understanding . . . and don't forget, they must be prayed for without ceasing. How is it that we think them crucial to our marital fulfillment?

Then there's the matter of economics. Children cost us so much money. A couple starts paying for them from the moment pregnancy seems like a possibility, and you keep paying for them until . . . until you decide to quit paying for them. You pay doctor bills and hospital bills that strap you for every dollar you've saved. You buy clothes and baby furniture and diapers and rattles and bottles and swing sets. You buy toys of every kind, shoes and more shoes. You pay for lessons they don't even want to take, braces, and antibiotics.

You have to help them crawl right and stand right and walk right. You have to move all your possessions out of their way. You have to bribe them and threaten them and tempt them. You guard them with your life, give them your last ounce of energy . . . and more of that praying for them without ceasing.

Raising kids is the hardest thing in the world! (If you don't have children, just ask your parents; they'll be glad to enlighten you.)

But I have to tell you that the happiest three days of our marriage were when Marylyn gave birth to those three kids. I've never been as proud in my life as I've been about those kids. If I had it to do all over again, I wouldn't change a thing. And I would gladly give every dime I have, and even my very life, if their lives depended on it.

When I look at those three girls today, what I'm wildest about is how much like their mother they are. And I can see some of me in them, too—some of Marylyn and me mixed together. Nothing in all my existence contributes nearly so much to my love for marriage as the idea that those three represent half of my genes and half of Marylyn's—all stirred together by the Creator himself.

Now, if I can just get them to obey the Ten Commandments, especially that middle one. And remember, whether you have children or are one, that commandment in the middle still applies.

> *Lord Jesus, we could never begin to thank you enough for children—or for our own parents. Thank you for the plan by which you entrust children to their parents for a few years. Answer the prayer of all parents that their children will be taken very good care of by you, surround them with your love, and fill them with your happy, healthy, wonderful Spirit. And give parents the strength and courage to continue to be parents—even after the children have grown up. Amen.*

HOLIDAY
BLUES

Dr. Kevin Leman

Remember the wonders he has done.

PSALM 105:5

*C*hristmas comes in many colors—the traditional red and green, the dreamy white, and unfortunately, the blues brought on by family conflict.

I believe young couples should establish their own holiday traditions as soon as possible. Instead of going to his parents' or her parents' home for Christmas or Thanksgiving, have the holidays at your own place. Invite your parents over for a change.

Holding out for practicing your own family traditions can be challenging. It can lead to friction, not only between the two of you but also with other relatives. One Christmas, after nearly twenty-five years of marriage, I experienced my own holiday "crisis."

Because I'm always eager to give my children a taste of their "Leman roots," I convinced the family it would be great to spend Christmas back in New York State. So we left sunny Tucson and were soon huddling around a roaring fireplace in the same cottage we live in during summer vacations, on the shores of Chautauqua Lake, not far from my sister Sally's home in Jamestown.

A few days after we arrived, I took my mother and Sally out to breakfast at a local restaurant. "I have a great idea," Sally announced. "Why don't you come to Grandpa's house for Christmas Eve?" They have always gathered at Grandpa's on Christmas Eve. By Grandpa, Sally meant her father-in-law. If we went, I'd feel like an intruder on her family's traditions.

Still, I thought about the suggestion for a couple of seconds before I pointed out that we were all going to have Christmas Day dinner at our cottage. I then mentioned that I preferred my hang-loose approach to Christmas Eve more than the structured evening Sally and her husband were comfortable with.

I pointed out that Sally's family would attend church services at eleven o'clock at night, but our three-year-old wouldn't take to going to church at that hour. Our Christmas Eve plans would include going to church early, around five, then coming home and having a casual buffet featuring turkey sandwiches. Then we would put on Christmas music, and if anyone had any final gift-wrapping to do, he or she would slip away to take care of it.

Sally didn't hear me. "But we want you to be there. Grandpa is going to read the Christmas story."

"Sally, we also read the Christmas story on Christmas Eve. I believe it's found in the book of Matthew and over in Luke as well. I think I'll read from Luke. I trust him more because he was a physician," I said with what I hoped was a twinkle in my eye.

My little attempt at humor died in midair, frozen in an icy wall of gloom. The rest of breakfast was quiet, with neither Mom nor Sally talking to me, but I stuck to my guns. I preferred risking disapproval, hurt feelings, and ruffled feathers to being forced to agree to something I knew my family wouldn't enjoy. What we do on Christmas Eve may not seem profound, but it's something we highly value.

It all worked out. Our family had its usual Christmas Eve, as did Sally's. Then, on Christmas Day, Sally's family came over for dinner, the children played together, the adults relaxed, and the proverbial good time was had by all. We had survived our Christmas crisis.

I believe every family is like a snowflake—different and unique. Every family needs its own way of doing things—its own traditions. If you haven't established yours, begin this year. Start to discuss what suits your family right now. And stick to your guns when friends and family develop plans for your holidays. Ultimately, it will keep your Christmas white rather than blue.

> *Lord, thank you for the family unit, and for the chance to create our special kind of memories that always will speak of love and togetherness to each person. Help us to evaluate what suits our family's "personality." And enable us to gently let others know this time is set apart for our traditions—and we'll be happy to share them. Amen.*

WHAT
MAKES A
HOUSE A HOME?

Les and Leslie Parrott

*"Do you see this woman? I came into your house. You did
not give me any water for my feet, but she wet my feet
with her tears and wiped them with her hair."*

LUKE 7:44

Half a dozen years ago we moved into a new house built in
an old Seattle neighborhood. We were fortunate to have
input on the floor plan so the house was built to our specifica-
tions. We chose everything from the doorknobs to the dish-
washer, from the paint on the walls to the kinds of pipes that
were in them. Little else, it seemed, was accomplished in our
lives during the months of construction.

The day Brian, our contractor, finally handed us the keys, we
walked though the front door and signed some papers he had
waiting for us on the gleaming kitchen countertop. Then we
shook his hand to say our good-byes, but before he climbed into
his pickup to leave, he asked, "How long will it take you to make
this house a home?"

The answer seemed obvious to us: the day we move in. That is, until we thought about it a little longer.

"Maybe when we decorate it with things we enjoy," Leslie suggested. "Or maybe when we have kids and begin to raise our family in these rooms."

We never really came to a conclusion the day our contractor posed the question, but we thought about it, off and on, for years. Over time we decided that our house feels most like a home when we put into practice God's principles for loving each other within it. And we've learned in the last few years that the best way to do that is to focus on being a loving person. Surprise, that doesn't necessarily mean doing loving things but instead focusing on a loving attitude by spending time with Jesus.

Martha is the classic biblical example of someone who didn't quite get it. She opened her home to Jesus and his disciples, scurrying about to make mealtime preparations while her sister, Mary, sat and conversed with Jesus. Finally Martha complained.

"'Lord, don't you care that my sister has left me to do the work by myself? Tell her to help me!' 'Martha, Martha,' the Lord answered, 'you are worried and upset about many things, but only one thing is needed. Mary has chosen what is better, and it will not be taken away from her'" (Luke 10:40–42).

Martha was more concerned with doing loving things in the kitchen than being a loving person based on her relationship with Jesus. She was attending to everyone else's needs, but she didn't recognize her own need to sit at our Savior's feet. If she had, she then could have gone about her work with a whole different view of what's important.

The same is often true in our homes. We think that loving each other is all about doing things that are needed to keep a house running, when the most loving thing we can do is to sit at

Jesus' feet, especially together as husband and wife. When we concentrate on God together, the to-do list falls to the wayside, our priorities get straightened out, and we focus on the really important thing—loving God and each other. No doubt about it—that's when our house is most like a home.

Father, we want our marriage to be engulfed by love—your love. And we know that the best way to make that happen is to spend time together, not doing, but being in your presence. Teach us to rest in you. Help us make our home everything you want it to be.

REMEMBER THE TIME . . . ?

Paul Johnson

> *O daughters of Jerusalem, I charge you—if you find*
> *my lover, what will you tell him? Tell him*
> *I am faint with love.*
>
> SONG OF SONGS 5:8

Have you been to a wedding recently? If so, did you find yourself recounting with your partner the stories of your wedding day? Did it cause you to snuggle a little bit closer, to hold hands a little bit tighter, and to look at one another with gratefulness?

In August, Nicole and I attended a wedding that took place in a city a couple of hours away from Nashville. The drive gave Nicole and me time to reminisce about our own wedding day and what we were doing at that particular point in our day.

After the wedding, we drove to the home of Nicole's dad for a family celebration, where once again we had a chance to relive the wedding memories and laugh over the good ones, grimace over the sad ones. In fact, Nicole's family is great about that kind of thing . . .

In the future, when your son asks you, "What is the meaning of the stip-
ulations, decrees and laws the LORD our God has commanded you?" tell him:
"We were slaves of Pharaoh in Egypt, but the LORD brought us out of Egypt
with a mighty hand" (Deuteronomy 6:20–21).

Every summer, Nicole's father's extended family gathers for
a prayer retreat. About forty to fifty people, who span three generations, attend. They pray for one another, express gratitude to
the Lord for his blessing and deliverance, and tell stories. The
highlight of the weekend is Saturday night, when family members recount memories and spouses recall stories about coming
into the family. The evening is redolent with stories, laughter,
more stories, more laughter. If any lulls occur, another pot of coffee is put on, and once it's ready, we go again. During most of
the weekend, the kids are off doing their own Bible study, but
for that evening, they are ensconced on their parents' laps, listening and laughing right along . . .

We will not hide them from their children; we will tell the next generation
the praiseworthy deeds of the LORD, his power, and the wonders he has done
(Psalm 78:4).

Families need to pass on their stories—like the time
Grandma ended up facedown in the potato salad at the family
picnic or the one about Dad forgetting the toilet paper on the
camping trip. Such tales help families draw closer together
through shared memories. As cherished stories are told over and
over again, they weave the threads of a family tighter. An ever-
evolving tapestry forms as the family shares the fabric of its life
from generation to generation . . .

The man said to me, "Son of man, look with your eyes and hear with your
ears and pay attention to everything I am going to show you, for that is why you
have been brought here. Tell the house of Israel everything you see" (Ezekiel 40:4).

Have you noticed that, when relatives come to your house,
the most treasured moments are when you all sit around the

living room or family room, everyone with his or her cup of coffee, tea, or hot chocolate? The hours pass away as you roar with laughter over your stories. A deeper sense of family is instilled as you come to know each other via each other's stories . . .

On that day tell your son, "I do this because of what the LORD did for me when I came out of Egypt" (Exodus 13:8).

If you are a parent, you want your kids to remember important stuff like jumping into big piles of fall leaves or feeling the cold snap of winter air while sipping hot chocolate. So jot a reminder on the calendar to make those fall and winter memories happen. And while you're sitting with calendar in hand, plan a year's worth of memory-making events that span the seasons. Strong memories are the durable fabric of marriages and close families . . .

Jesus . . . said, "Go home to your family and tell them how much the Lord has done for you, and how he has had mercy on you" (Mark 5:19).

Our Savior Jesus, you used stories to convey your love to our broken world. May we recount with gladness our lives' stories that our hope might be renewed and that our faith might remain strong in you.

Part Four
Celebrating Our Oneness

THE BLUE CHIP MARRIAGE INVESTMENT

Les and Leslie Parrott

Above all, love each other deeply, because love
covers over a multitude of sins.

1 PETER 4:8

We have a friend who always is thinking of innovative ways to show his wife how much he loves her. On one occasion he ordered a pizza for their Friday night at home in front of the television. But this wasn't your ordinary pizza. He asked for the hand-tossed crust to be shaped like a heart and outlined in pepperoni pieces. And he didn't stop there. He asked for extra anchovies all over the pie—he hates anchovies, but his wife loves them.

The pizza parlor manager was so impressed with this guy's romantic creativity, the manager not only made the pizza himself, but he also delivered it—and he told the lovebirds the pizza was on the house. He then took a couple of photos to hang on the wall of his shop and then, before leaving, said, "Either you two are some of the most romantic people I've ever met, or your husband is in really big trouble."

Isn't that true? When your spouse goes the extra mile to say "I love you," does a part of you wonder if something's up? Do you reflexively brace yourself for bad news? Or do you have the kind of relationship in which out-of-the-ordinary expressions of love are an ordinary way of life?

If you're like most couples, you don't receive many heart-shaped pizzas. In fact, one of the most common complaints of married couples, especially wives, is that they miss the little expressions of appreciation and love that meant so much when they were dating. They now feel taken for granted. What's worse, they probably are.

As the weeks turn into months, and months into years, and years into decades, it's easy to assume your spouse knows how much you care for him or her. But that's a mistake. It's an assumption that quietly siphons off your love life. It depletes the amount of connection between husband and wife, that sense of oneness.

Some experts call the sense of togetherness a love bank or an emotional tank. They are referring to the emotional bank account that resides within your spouse, the metaphorical place where you make emotional deposits and withdrawals. It's a great analogy because every one of us, every day, withdraws emotional energy from our spouse when we are insensitive or selfish. And when the balance in the account runs dangerously low, each infraction is magnified because no reserves of trust and appreciation exist against which to make withdrawals. What's worse, we may be living on borrowed capital, and each additional withdrawal pushes our marriage toward bankruptcy.

Perhaps this is part of what Peter is getting at when he says, "Above all, love each other deeply, because love covers over a multitude of sins." When your partner's emotional bank account has a high balance, when you have loved each other deeply, your marital "sins" are almost overlooked by your partner.

So the question is, what are you doing to love each other deeply? Our friends who ordered the romantic pizza have a special way they express their love for one another in the winter months. When they go to bed, the one who crawls between the sheets first will lie on the other person's side of the bed for a few minutes to warm it up. After all, who doesn't like crawling into a warm bed on a cold night? It's a little thing, but each of them is constantly looking for ways to say "I love you." Each time they do, they are increasing the emotional wealth of their marriage.

You can do the same thing. Even if you think you're romantically impaired, think back to your dating days. Remember how you went out of your way to woo your partner? You have it in you, it's simply a matter of making a choice to love each other deeply. And the rewards of togetherness are great.

Lord, keep us from being overdrawn on our emotional bank accounts with each other. Help us to make deposits by remembering to do the little things that say "I love you." Give us the desire to build up our love account to overflowing. And remind us that it is your love within us that enables us to set aside our selfish desires and love each other the way we really want to.

A New
Name

Rachael Crabb

> *You will be called by a new name that the
> mouth of the LORD will bestow.*
>
> ISAIAH 62:2

You have to really be in love to *want* to be called Mrs.
Crabb. I was eager to assume that new identity from early
on in my relationship with Larry.

We met when we were ten years old but didn't begin to date
until we were twelve (he's exactly three weeks older than I). I
remember telling my mom that I was in love with Larry Crabb
and going to marry him someday. She replied, "I don't want to
hear about it until you're eighteen years old."

That wasn't the response I wanted, but one I knew I could
work around—at least every seventh Saturday at lunchtime. You
see, each Saturday one of the seven members of my family had
the opportunity to pick a seafood item for lunch. When it was
my turn, I always said, "I love crab." Actually, I didn't care for
crabmeat, but I had a point to make.

Finally, the morning of my eighteenth birthday, I ran down the steps in our home shouting, "Mother, I'm in love with Larry Crabb, and I'm going to marry him!"

About eighteen days after I received my Bachelor of Science degree in elementary education, Larry could no longer call himself a bachelor, for we were married, and I found the name "Crabb" a most effective one for a schoolteacher. After our honeymoon we settled in Champaign, Illinois, where I taught fourth grade and where Larry entered his second year of graduate school in clinical psychology. I don't know if the schoolchildren will remember a thing I taught, but I do know they'll remember my name.

I still enjoy my "new" name, and the many griefs and blessings that come from being a Crabb.

I was given another new name a few years before I became a Crabb, and that name is known by God. As the verse for today in Isaiah says, "You will be called by a new name that the mouth of the LORD will bestow." By trusting Jesus Christ's death on the cross as payment for my sins, I am given a new name.

In your marriage, you might or might not have acquired a new name, but you certainly acquired a new identity. The use of one name for two people is, of course, a symbolic expression of the union that you have formed with each other. A most perfect union in which two people blended into one another until neither knew where one ended and the other began.

The nicknames you call each other hold tremendous meaning, too. "Sweetie," "Honeybun," and even "Spud" are terms of endearment that not everyone feels an inclination to use regarding their spouse. "Hey you" doesn't hold a candle to "Dimples"—as long as you aren't referring to a cellulite condition! And "Sweetheart" spoken through gritted teeth doesn't communicate the same loving spirit as when that name is whispered softly.

The names you call each other contain much power to move you closer together or to pull you apart. And the names you use are indicative of the state of your union. Concentrate on using endearing names. And be inventive. New names enhance our sense of oneness—sometimes even when they are "Mrs. Crabb."

> *Dear Lord, thank you for the new names you give to us both in marriage and in spirit. Help us to bestow loving names on each other and not to resort to name calling. And, Lord, we want you to know that we look forward to hearing our names when we see you face to face, when, as your bride, our marriage with you will be celebrated.*

THREE-MINUTE CONNECTION

Becky and Roger Tirabassi

Therefore, as God's chosen people, holy and dearly loved,
clothe yourselves with compassion, kindness, humility,
gentleness and patience. Bear with each other and forgive
whatever grievances you may have against one another.
Forgive as the Lord forgave you.

COLOSSIANS 3:12–13

I happen to live with a man who counsels engaged and married couples for a living. Though I've often joked that God saved me a lot of professional fees by allowing me to marry a counselor, I have received the benefit of the valuable communication skills and principles Roger teaches to couples.

One of the most practical techniques that Roger encourages couples to incorporate into their daily lives is called the "3 A's." It's a daily, three-minute exercise that encourages couples to connect with each other physically, emotionally, and spiritually by following a simple pattern.

Each partner shares an *affirmation*, an *apology*, and an *affection*. At a designated point in the day—whether just before you slip into bed at night or at the start of the day—each person takes a turn to express the 3 A's.

Affirmation: Share one way that your partner has helped you during the day (such as going to the store for you, driving the car pool, or making dinner) or one aspect of your mate's life that you admire (such as patience or kindness exhibited during the day).

Apology: Ask your partner, "Is there any way that I hurt you today?" After the partner shares any hurt in a brief sentence or two, the one who asked replies, "Will you forgive me for hurting you in that way?" (Note: This is not the time for conflict resolution, though an appointment for one might be necessary. This is time to briefly express something that might not otherwise be communicated.)

Affection: Offer a hug, soft kiss, toe-touch, or back rub for this brief moment of physical touch, though it certainly might lead to more intimacy!

As a bonus *A*, I like to encourage couples to close their daily connection time with "Amen," a prayer for each other and their kids.

By design, the 3 A's are meant to allow a couple to connect with each other whether the day has been difficult or easy, sad or joyous. It's not intended to be a session for hashing out differences or resolving deep hurts. Those sessions need to be planned for at mutually agreed upon times, as well as carefully facilitated.

Do the 3 A's really work? In our home, we don't always manage to express the 3 A's every day, but we do the exercise a few times a week at the end of the day. Because I'm more of the initiator, I'm often the one who suggests it's time for the 3 A's, especially if we've experienced a bit of conflict.

One night recently we went to bed after a disagreement. As we settled under the covers, I asked, "Would you like to do the 3 A's?"

Roger had rolled over so I couldn't see his face. That was unusual behavior for him so I asked again but received no response.

"Have you fallen asleep or are you pretending?"

No reply.

The first thing I did in the morning was walk around to his side of the bed so I could see his face, and I gently patted him on the shoulder to wake him.

The moment his eyes opened, I asked, "Were you sleeping last night when I asked if you wanted to do the 3 A's, or were you pretending?"

He looked at me sheepishly ... and confessed his stubbornness.

I smiled and replied, "Would you kindly tell your counselees today that you refused to do the 3 A's last night?"

He chuckled, and our humorous exchange broke the ice. We took the time necessary to resolve our differences and heal our hurts.

This little exercise not only gives us a fun way to connect regularly with each other, but it also provides a forum for us to recognize when we have unresolved problems and need to take the time to deal with them.

Like taking a daily vitamin pill as preventive medicine, please consider incorporating the 3 A's into your relationship.

> *Lord, give us the desire to affirm, to apologize, and to be genuinely affectionate with each other on a daily basis. Cause our love for each other to be a reflection of your love toward us. Help us to make time every day to connect with you and each other.*

Team
Huddle

Neil Clark Warren

Then they cast lots, and the lot fell to Matthias;
so he was added to the eleven apostles.

Acts 1:26

I've studied thousands of marriages, and the best ones by far are the ones that build teamwork into the center of them. The power of these marriages is the result of the reverberating and multiplying effects of two people bringing out the best in each other. Instead of 1 + 1, these marriages operate with the power of 2 x 2.

We all know how much emphasis Jesus placed on teamwork. If a world was going to be won, every person needed to do his or her job. There were the twelve apostles, the seventy disciples, and the eventual elders and deacons. There were the women who ministered to Jesus, and the women whose money made it all possible, and the men and women who believed so passionately that they sacrificed their lives for the power of the witness it gave. They were all part of the team, and every person's role was defined and desperately important. And what an amazing team it was!

Your marriage and mine will succeed or fail depending on the precision of our teamwork. For instance, Marylyn and I are having another couple over for dinner tonight. Since we have an afternoon full of other commitments, we'll need to work fast and efficiently. After all these years together, we know pretty much everything that needs to be done. I'll buy the steaks, and she'll fix the salad. I'll clean the table on the patio, light the barbecue, and set the table. She'll cook a vegetable, prepare a dessert. You know what I mean. The evening will be ten times as enjoyable if Marylyn and I do our various duties as part of a team.

Five principles will guide our team's functioning. First, we need to huddle and get our signals straight. Every required detail needs to be assigned to one of us, and we each need to know exactly what we're expected to do.

Second, we need to agree on what's most important for the evening to be a success. For instance, making our friends feel welcome and well taken care of may well be our number-one goal. From start to finish, their enjoyment and satisfaction will likely be our focused objective.

Third, Marylyn and I do our best when we stay in close communication during the evening. I really like it when we touch each other a lot, and she really likes it when I stay verbally positive and enthusiastic.

Fourth, we do best when we watch each other's eyes for cues. Sometimes Marylyn wants me to offer our guests some more water or to pass the meat again. She really appreciates my staying alert to gentle cues so that she doesn't have to break into the conversation.

Finally, Marylyn and I soar as teammates when we compliment each other generously. Nothing means quite so much as the other team member's reinforcement and encouragement.

In Acts 1, at the disciples' very first meeting after Jesus had ascended into heaven, they set about appointing the last team member, the one to replace Judas. They prayed about it, and they treated the matter of the "team lineup" with great seriousness.

The makeup of your team is critical, too. But once you have chosen the person you want to team with, your all-consuming challenge is to work together enthusiastically to reach your goals.

Boy, marriage sure goes a lot better when there's plenty of team pride. And remember the principles that work so well for Marylyn and me: Get the right teammate, settle on your goals, assign every detail to one of you, keep your communication frequent and subtle, encourage each other every chance you get, and then celebrate the victories.

You want to know how this dinner for our friends is going to go tonight? Having just rehearsed the game plan by writing this devotional, my guess is that I'll be an absolute all-star for our team. Of course, if I do my job right, Marylyn will end up feeling like an all-star as well. That's the way it is with teammates, and being teammates makes for great evenings—and marriages that last forever.

> Lord Jesus, thank you for making each of us a part of this marital team. Help us to believe in the extra power that can be ours when we work closely together in pursuit of our common objectives. Please forgive the overzealousness that causes one of us to act like he or she is the coach, the captain, and the star. May we each excitedly share the decision-making and the work, the happy outcomes, and the crushing defeats. We both want so much to be on a great team, but we need your help and encouragement every step of the way. In Jesus' name. Amen.

Money
Matters
in Marriage

Les and Leslie Parrott

Do not store up for yourselves treasures on earth, where
moth and rust destroy, and where thieves break in and steal.
But store up for yourselves treasures in heaven, where moth and
rust do not destroy, and where thieves do not break in and steal. For
where your treasure is, there your heart will be also.

Matthew 6:19–21

We were at home getting ready for dinner, half-tuned into the local television news broadcast, when our ears pricked up. It was a report on a unique wedding. In our years of counseling countless newlywed couples, we've seen or heard of numerous bizarre ceremonies: Getting married on a roller coaster, while scuba diving, and so on. But the one in this evening's news report took the cake. Literally.

Tom Anderson and his bride, Sabrina Root, paid for their recent $34,000 wedding—cake and all—by selling advertising space at the ceremony and reception. Everything from the wedding rings to a week at a penthouse in Cancun, Mexico, was donated after the couple persuaded nearly two dozen companies to sponsor the nuptials in exchange for having their names appear six times, from the invitation to the thank-you cards. The bride drew the line at having advertising banners draped across the aisle, but her perfume came from a local Oscar de la Renta distributor, and the coffee was provided gratis by a neighborhood supplier.

After seeing the report on this wedding, each of us had a different response. Leslie: "How tacky." Les: "Not a bad idea." It provided enough fodder for a complete dinner discussion that night. But we still ended up, at least for argument's sake, holding to our differing views.

Whatever you think about this couple's fiscal scheme for launching their marriage, you have to admit one thing: Tom and Sabrina, whether they planned to or not, discussed their money matters more than most couples about to be married. And that's not a bad thing.

Did you know that money is the number-one source of conflict in marriage? More than any other issue, couples fight about finances. And with good reason. The dollar serves as a weapon for some people. It provides a potential battleground for disputes over responsibility and judgment. Why? Because we don't talk about it. We may argue about it, but we don't *talk* about it.

It's hard for most couples to discuss money matters. Yet Jesus spoke about money more frequently than any other subject except the kingdom of God. His careful attention to financial issues is one of the amazing aspects about the Gospel narratives. The range of his concern is startling: from the parable of the sower (Matthew 13:22) to the parable of the rich farmer (Luke 12:16–21), from the encounter with the rich young ruler (Matthew 19:16–23) to the encounter with Zacchaeus, the rich tax collector (Luke 19), from teachings on trust in Matthew 6:25–34 to teachings on the danger of wealth in Luke 6:24–25.

The point is, we couples need to talk about money. And keep talking about it. Some of us need to give up being money monks who have taken a vow of silence about family finances. Others of us need to pipe down and speak in a calm voice that invites our partner to open up. Money matters in marriage. And the more we talk about it, the more likely we are to honor God with our financial decisions and to feel like a truly united couple—in every way.

Heavenly Father, help us to keep money in perspective. While it often seems we don't have enough, keep us from taking our financial frustrations out on each other. Help us to talk through our concerns and expectations about our finances and to remember we are a unit, we are for each other, and neither of us is the enemy. Remind us that all our blessings come from you. Amen.

TRUE
LOVE

Gary Smalley

Love must be sincere. Hate what is evil; cling to what
is good. Be devoted to one another in brotherly love.
Honor one another above yourselves.

ROMANS 12:9–10

Being a so-called "relationship expert" carries with it certain expectations. For example, I should understand how to repair my mistakes with my wife, Norma, in such a way that harmony will return to our relationship. Most of the time I'm up to the challenge, but sometimes I fall flat on my face.

Like the time I tried to be the consummate nineties man, and I set off to do a load of laundry for my hardworking wife. I thought I could earn some bonus points by doing her laundry, which, I might add, she forbade me ever to do because of my long-standing track record of ruining her clothes. This particular load of laundry consisted of some of my wife's favorite outfits. Perhaps that fact alone should have given me pause . . .

As the wash cycle ended, I remembered Norma saying she didn't leave her clothes in the dryer too long so as to avoid shrinkage. So I made a mental note as I threw her clothes into the dryer, but I didn't set the timer. Perhaps that fact should have given me pause . . .

Two hours later I remembered the clothes. Norma had just returned home from work, and as I greeted her at the door, the sight of her warm smile jostled my memory. I quickly excused myself and darted downstairs.

How would I explain to Norma that I had cooked her clothes?

"Norm," I announced as I sauntered into the kitchen, "I have good news and bad news, which would you like to hear first?"

Norma likes the bad news first, so I calmly explained that her favorite wardrobe was shrunk.

"What?" She bolted down to the laundry room. As I trailed behind her, I reminded her that I also had good news. After examining her clothes, she asked, "What could possibly be the good news?"

I replied, "The good news is that we have a brand-new wardrobe for Taylor!" (Our five-year-old granddaughter.)

It was then that I thought about how sometimes Norma really doesn't have much of a sense of humor. Instead of laughing, she explained to me how hard it is to find just the right outfit and that it had taken her years to find the clothes I had ruined in one drying cycle.

I felt horrible but learned a couple of valuable lessons. First, don't ever wash your wife's clothes; it can't possibly do you any good.

Second, and most important, validate your wife's feelings. I could have shot back that material things shouldn't be so important, that Norma should be more concerned with spiritual things. I could have blasted back that I was just trying to help, and she should appreciate a husband who's willing to wash clothes. But neither of those comments would have helped our marriage.

To make my marriage the best, I needed to validate my mate's feelings, even though I didn't agree with her response and even though I felt embarrassed about what I had done. I needed to say, "I understand how valuable the clothes were to you and how hard you had shopped to find just the right pieces. I'm so sorry I ruined them. All we can do now is replace them. How can I help you find time to go shopping as soon as possible?" (Now, trust me, I was putting myself way out on the limb to ask that question—I could end up in the kitchen cooking up a disaster before I knew it!)

But the point is that validating how your spouse feels tells her that she is important—in fact, even more important than you are. Such an action reflects Christ's selfless love for us. When you validate your mate, you put his or her needs above your own.

Make an effort to let your spouse know you understand how he or she feels about a touchy issue today. (And if you *don't* know how your mate feels, find out.) All it takes is a little bit of effort and choosing to love your partner—and that's when true love is expressed in marriage.

> Lord, give us the strength to put our mate's needs above our own, which is something that goes against every fiber of our natural being. We want to honor our spouse, and we want to honor you in our relationship. Help us to express true love, just as you do toward us each day.

A GOOD
RETURN

Becky and Roger Tirabassi

*Two are better than one, because they have
a good return for their work.*

ECCLESIASTES 4:9

I first met Roger when I volunteered in the youth program he directed. We immediately found our working relationship compatible and fun. In fact, Roger identified my "call" and spiritual gift as an evangelist. He even encouraged me to go into ministry full-time.

After working together for a year, Roger asked me to marry him. As he "popped the question," he said, "I don't want to ruin our ministry relationship by dating." Because I was a relatively new believer, I remember thinking, "Oh, is this how Christians do it?" We had never kissed or dated; yet I said yes to his proposal.

One year and ten days later, we had our only child, Jacob. Starting with the first stage of parenthood, Roger and I always looked at our lives based on these priorities: parenting, our individual "call to ministry," our finances, our spiritual gifts, our work responsibilities and commitments, and the time available in a day.

Roger considered our marriage as a team. He believed the work we did together was more effective than the work we did alone. He felt strongly that "two are better than one" and that we would have a good, perhaps even better, return for our work if we tackled it as a team.

While many around us encouraged me to be an "at-home" mom, we considered my contributions to the youth organization with which we worked to be of great value. So we constantly adjusted our schedules to accommodate my new life as a mom. I opted to volunteer many hours rather than receive pay so I could continue my ministry with high school kids but have the flexibility to work out of my home or not to attend a meeting if it wasn't a good fit with our son's schedule. And, a few times each week, a relative or a friend watched Jake when I had a special event or meeting that wasn't appropriate for a toddler to attend. When Jacob went to kindergarten, I trooped off to the office in the mornings and continued to maintain an at-home office.

After we both were hired to work at the same church in California, we looked at our family and ministry commitments in light of the job offer. Roger was perfectly suited for the full-time position of director of the youth ministries program, but we determined I should work part-time so I would be available to Jake at 3 P.M. when he came home from school. We also negotiated for me to have reduced hours in the summer, when Jake wouldn't be in school.

By the time Jacob entered junior high, we had another big decision to make. I was beginning to be asked to speak for groups that were out of town. Because we always had considered our marriage a partnership—a team—we once again evaluated how we could continue to have a parent at home before and after school and on weekends during all of Jake's school years. After much prayer and consideration, Roger resigned from his full-time position and, over the next six years, forged a part-time pastoral counseling practice that allowed him to be the at-home parent until our son graduated from high school.

Each year we allow our spiritual gifts and call to ministry to guide the course we chart for our marriage and our family. Even though our lives haven't followed a traditional pattern, after twenty-one years of marriage and twenty of parenthood, we've concluded that "two are better than one, because they have a good return for their work."

I've rehearsed for you the course Roger's life and mine have taken together to encourage you to be willing, as a couple, to lean in and listen to what God is calling you to do, not to follow the worn path but to tread the road he leads you to. And to remember, whatever you do, that the two of you will do it better than one of you could have.

Lord, thank you for bringing us together and for giving us different gifts and abilities so that, as a team, we have a good return for our work. Help us encourage each other to use our gifts and to be wise stewards of our time and abilities. Help us to express to each other how important each is to the whole.

Speaking from the Heart

Gary Smalley

> *Let love and faithfulness never leave you;*
> *bind them around your neck, write them on*
> *the tablet of your heart.*
>
> PROVERBS 3:3

Many years ago a preacher decided to sell his mountain trail horse. A prospective buyer was impressed with the animal's skill and obedience. Before they agreed on a price the preacher said, "I must warn you he only responds to spiritual commands. To get the horse moving you say, 'Praise the Lord,' and 'Stop' is 'Hallelujah.'"

"I've been around horses all my life," said the buyer, "and I've never heard of such a thing." Mounting the horse, he said skeptically, "Praise the Lord." The horse began to trot. He repeated, "Praise the Lord," and the horse broke into a gallop. Suddenly the buyer realized a cliff was dead ahead. Frantically he yelled, "Hallelujah," and they came to a stop a foot from the edge. Wiping the sweat from his brow, the buyer said, "Praise the Lord!"

Often we feel like that buyer when it comes to repairing the mistakes we make with our spouse. Our intentions are good, but we just seem to end up saying the wrong thing. How do we make amends for our wrongs?

First, approach your spouse softly and tenderly after hurting his or her feelings. Tenderness provides an atmosphere in which your partner can think clearly because he or she doesn't have to erect defenses.

Second, understand, as much as possible, what your spouse is feeling. Empathize with your mate. That validates your spouse's feelings. When your mate closes his or her spirit to you, more often than not, that person wants you to acknowledge the hurt you've caused.

Third, seek forgiveness. That generally starts with taking ownership of your mistakes. If you start to blame your spouse, that invalidates any request for forgiveness. And understand that forgiveness is a process; your mate might not respond immediately, but in time he or she will be ready to forgive.

Hurt feelings are impossible to avoid in marriage. We live in an imperfect world with imperfect marriages. The incredible thing is that God can turn these moments of pain into gems of intimacy. If we repair our mistakes by expressing from our heart tenderness and understanding and by seeking forgiveness, we'll experience deeper intimacy because, as a couple, we'll have grown closer together through our trials and tribulation.

As Proverbs says, "Let love and faithfulness never leave you; bind them around your neck, write them on the tablet of your heart." Love and faithfulness are found in the heart of one who is willing to learn, willing to be soft, and willing to take ownership of his or her own failures. When you find that place within yourself, then you're ready to speak from your heart.

Lord, help each of us to seek understanding with an open mind, an open heart, and a humble spirit that only desires to follow your will and to love one another. Teach us that intimacy with one another comes from faithfully working to be tender and forgiving.

Part Five

Celebrating—Even in
Tough Times

What the
Mamas and
the Papas Never Saw

Nicole Johnson

*Therefore we do not lose heart. Though outwardly we
are wasting away, yet inwardly we are being renewed day
by day. For our light and momentary troubles are achieving
for us an eternal glory that far outweighs them all.*

2 Corinthians 4:16–17

I stared out our rental car window at the brown leaves sticking
to the wet pavement of a Portland street. It was still raining
slightly, and it was bitterly cold. I thought, *I could never live here.*
Gray, damp, and cold get to me after, oh, about twenty minutes.
With all the leaves brown, and the sky one big shade of gray, I
definitely started "California dreaming," as the Mamas and the
Papas described the longing for fair weather in one of their
songs.

I took the memory of that day with me the second time we
landed in Oregon. This time the trees were not brown, and the
sky was not gray. Instead the place looked as if every tree in the
state was on fire. The horizon literally was glowing with the
richest hues I had ever seen. The golds, oranges, and reds

seemed brighter than anything that had ever come off the end of a painter's brush. The total view, as well as each individual tree, was breathtaking, and I scarcely could take it in.

Well, my attitude toward the city did a complete reversal, and I became an unofficial employee of the Portland Tourist Bureau. I told friends everywhere how beautiful the leaves were, and how everyone should plan a visit if they were ever going to be in the area—and even if they weren't.

Several people asked, "Haven't you seen leaves turn colors before?"

Reminding them I live in Tennessee and that, yes, our leaves do change colors, I assured them our southern leaves didn't look like the leaves I had seen in Portland. But I wondered why.

Then, two years ago, we traveled to New England. Magnificent leaves created a stunning landscape of fire. I saw again the intense beauty of a tree surrendering to change, of nature painting a glorious picture of the cycle of living and dying. And once again I was left breathless by the brightness and vividness.

Eventually I figured out that we don't have leaves like that in Tennessee because we don't have winters like that. The colder weather makes the colors glow. The trees are crowned in honor for all they suffer. The winter produces the fire. And then I saw it everywhere . . .

She was forty-two years old when the cancer came. His love for her never faltered. Through chemotherapy and the accompanying hair loss and sickness, their marriage grew stronger. He took time off from work and became a student in the school of his wife's needs. They've won the battle against cancer so far, and the color of success is stunning. The leaves are brighter because the winter is harder . . .

Many couples lose their marriages when a company they've poured their lives into goes bankrupt. But when he broke the news that after twenty profitable years in business there would be no more, she assured him there would be. Standing together on the brink of financial ruin, they could see a glowing vista that very few others could. The colder weather makes the colors glow . . .

Their son was in jail. He had been picked up for possession of drugs and was sitting in a cell downtown. The accusations had gone back and forth between the couple, but there was nowhere to place the blame. At 2 A.M., together they bowed their knees, asking for forgiveness for what they had done wrong and for the grace to start over. Then, silent but united in spirit, they drove a short distance to face a long journey, hearts blazing with hope. The winter produces the fire.

Without exception, the couples we've known who have gone through the deepest struggles have the brightest leaves. They've walked bravely through the winters of their lives, bloomed in the spring, wilted with the rest of us in the summer, but come the fall, they are blazing! They live in the intense beauty of surrendering to change, allowing God to paint through them the cycle of living and dying. My breath is taken away by the vivid colors.

As you encounter the struggles of marriage, as you feel that outwardly you are wasting away, trust God that he is using his brush and your marital relationship to paint a magnificent landscape. From the middle of the hardest winters, believe that the greatest colors will come. And try to get to Portland if you can!

> Father, give us grace to believe that suffering will produce in us the colors that we long for in this gray world. Help us to trust your cycle of nature even when it feels that the winter will never end. And let us give you the glory in the fall of our lives when you shine through us and we simply reflect your radiance with blazing clarity. Amen.

WHEN GOD
HOLDS BACK

Larry Crabb

> *Then Naomi said, "Wait, my daughter, until you find*
> *out what happens. For the man will not rest until*
> *the matter is settled today."*
>
> RUTH 3:18

I love the story of Naomi. More than any other narrative in the Old Testament, this one has pulled me through especially tough times.

Naomi's story is told in the book of Ruth, named after Naomi's fiercely loyal daughter-in-law. After both women lost their husbands, these two widows moved to Naomi's hometown to live in poverty. But then, as luck would have it (or, if you see the real point of the story, as God arranged it), Ruth fell in love with an older man of considerable wealth named Boaz, one of Naomi's relatives. And he fell in love with Ruth. With such a marriage in sight, Naomi and Ruth knew they would be set for life. Good-bye, poverty! Hello, wealth!

But one little glitch could end everyone's hopes for happiness. Boaz realized that a technicality in Jewish law stood in the way of his marrying Ruth. He told her he would try to work things out.

Ruth panicked. Would her dreams come true? She couldn't be certain.

My favorite line in the entire story (well, *one* of my favorites) comes when Naomi speaks to Ruth from Naomi's deeper knowledge of God and life. "Wait, my daughter, until you find out what happens. For the man will not rest until the matter is settled today" (3:18).

Wait! Is there a harder command to follow? Every marriage, every family, every life faces tough times, moments when the outcome is uncertain. Wait, while your heart is being ripped to shreds. Wait, when a bad outcome would throw your life into unspeakable pain.

Maybe your husband ignores you—sometimes in subtle ways, sometimes in very obvious ways. Wait for God to work, maybe adjusting your husband's receptivity, maybe giving you the strength to handle the minimizing effects of his behavior. Maybe your wife never sees her contributions to your tensions. It's always *your* fault. Wait till God builds in you the humility, patience, and wisdom to be strong, even loving.

But how do we wait? Our frantic determination to have things the way they should be *now* reflects our terror that no one really cares about what is happening to us, at least no one who can do anything about it.

Naomi told Ruth to wait, but then Naomi added, "The man will not rest until the matter is settled today." Naomi knew Boaz wanted to marry Ruth and to make her life (and Naomi's) better.

Here's the point—not Naomi's point perhaps, but the lesson we can learn today. Jesus Christ longs to bless us, but right now he is holding himself back from pouring every blessing he can think of into our lives. One day he will, but for now he is restraining himself for good purposes we can't always see.

He's like a wealthy, generous father who wisely knows the new sports car his teenage son wants might not be a good idea. So the father holds himself back to achieve better purposes in his son that, for the life of him, the son can't see and might not value even if he could.

You won't wait well (you might not wait at all) unless you catch a glimpse of God's loving heart. He is not indifferent, callous, or cruel. Look hard at the cross and realize that Jesus would go to that extreme to give you a life worth living. How could he withhold any good thing after giving his life?

Answer? He wouldn't. He doesn't. He isn't. It just looks that way. He is more eager to bless than we are to be blessed. Waiting is our expression of trust, of believing he is truly good.

I suspect heaven will be more fun for Jesus than for us, just like the parent who loves Christmas more than the kids. Giving *is* more fun than receiving. Till then, wait! What's coming is unbelievable.

Dear Lord, help each of us, in our areas of need, to see you, right now, restraining yourself from giving what we want. Help us to realize that you long to bless us fully and that one day you will. Teach us patience and trust so we can love well—both you and each other—even in the middle of difficult times. Lord, teach us to wait, patiently, hopefully, and quietly.

I'm Going Bonkers!

Dr. Kevin Leman

*The LORD replied, "My Presence will go with
you, and I will give you rest."*

EXODUS 33:14

A harried-looking woman, dragging her leg as if she had
some sort of neurological disorder, limped into my office
one day. As she plopped down on the sofa, I noted that the reason for her odd gait was an eighteen-month-old who was clinging to her skirt like a leech.

The woman's first words were, "Can you help me, Dr. Leman?
I'm going bonkers!"

She was a classic prototype of the stressed-out wife and
mom. She was trying hard to be a good mother to four children
while balancing everything else as well: her husband, a full-time
job, and three or four other assignments she had taken on from
the PTA, her church, and the cerebral palsy campaign.

Her story is the story of so many women who wind up in my
office. The candidate for Bonkersville comes trudging home
from her job and fixes dinner. After hubby and the children have

all eaten, she cleans up the kitchen. Then she stops to pick up the family room and living room. Next, she irons something for tomorrow, packs some lunches, and finally heads for the bedroom, where she hopes to read a few pages of her mystery novel or turn on the eleven o'clock news. There she is, propped up on her pillows, reaching for her book or the TV guide, and *he* walks in with a look that reminds her of Pavlov's dog and the power of operant conditioning. She spots his salivating smile and the glint in his eyes and groans, "Oh, no, not, not, not—no, no, no—not one more chore!"

Poor hubby. He doesn't realize it, but his wife has just erected her own little neon sign that reads, "Don't even think of parking here." Most women would rather scrub the toilet than engage in sex at 10:55 at night after working all day, cooking dinner, cleaning up, putting the kids to bed, and making sure everything is ready for tomorrow.

Our stressed-out woman doesn't realize it, but she is a victim of the tyranny of the urgent. The urgent tasks of her day have crowded out the important things—including hubby and his salivating smile. Of course, since hubby hasn't done his part, all he'll get to do tonight is salivate. He could have insured himself a much warmer welcome to bed if he had helped her clean up the kitchen, pick up the house, and bathe and bed down the kids for the night. But he was too busy watching the Monday night gladiators of the gridiron. After all, he has certain "urgent" things in his life, too.

Attention all husbands: Your wife can't keep your family together all by herself. You must play an active role in helping to sort out the urgent and the important and then do your share of both.

Husbands' sex lives will improve 300 percent if they'll just do some of the little chores in life, like taking out the garbage without being asked, carting the kids to school, being more attentive to their mothers-in-law—or possibly, most important, changing their schedules.

A good plan for prioritizing is to label things A—must do, B—should do, or C—can do. But over and above that, you should label your marriage AAA—must do. In other words, your marriage is the highest priority of all. In fact, your marriage is much more than a "must do." It's do or disintegrate.

If your marriage is coming in a distant second, third, or fourth behind a lot of other priorities, you need to grapple with reality. And reality says that if you don't start doing things differently, you have an excellent chance of becoming one more statistic, one more small part of the giant average that says a marriage lasts some seven years and is gone.

In a word, you must prioritize, and that means your spouse must come first. When your marriage comes first, everything else falls into its proper place.

I realize this may be a strange idea for many wives and husbands. The hard-driving husband who is out there "breaking his neck for his wife and the kids" working sixty or seventy hours a week may find it just too hard to swallow. And it may seem impossible to a mom with three little ankle-biters who consume her twenty-four hours a day. Just where is she supposed to find all this time for her husband (assuming he's even around)?

Nonetheless, I stand by my top priority. For any couple—particularly the overly busy, hard-driving husbands and wives who are trying to juggle career and family—there are plenty of reasons to seek refuge in each other, to have some time for yourselves. Finding time for each other can be done—if you both really want to.

> Lord, life pulls at us from so many different directions. In the vortex of all the activity, give us creative ways to find rest with one another. Help us to hold onto each other rather than push each other away when too many demands call for our attention. Amen.

THE CAREFUL MANAGEMENT OF A BLAZING ANGER

Neil Clark Warren

> *Then the Lord said, "I have seen what a stubborn, rebellious lot these people are. Now let me alone and my anger shall blaze out against them and destroy them all; and I will make you, Moses, into a great nation instead of them."*
>
> EXODUS 32:9–10 LB

D r. David Mace, a prominent American marriage counselor, says that more marriages are destroyed because two people don't know how to handle their anger toward each other than for any other reason.

Anger finds different forms of expression. For instance, if you could have met my mother, I suspect you would have joined the chorus of people who thought Rosa Warren was one of the sweetest persons God ever created. One of nine children born to John and Iva Clark, Mom grew up on a farm in rural Iowa. She loved school, but the country schools of her day only went through the eighth grade. When she was seventeen, my mother met and married my dad, Otis James Warren, a big, bright, hard-working businessman who purchased a grocery store when he was seventeen, got married at nineteen, and went on to own one business after another.

Otis Warren was a kind, generous man, but he was a much stronger person than the woman he married. In the spirit of the times, he was the king of their home, and he controlled her, their three children, and nearly everyone else he encountered.

For all the world, had you known them, you would have thought that she dealt with his controlling nature quite well. She was nurturing to her children, kind to her family of origin, and a stalwart of the country church they attended. But with my psychologist's eye, I can look back and see how much emotional pain she experienced.

Primary pain, you see, is at the root of all anger. This pain involves hurt, frustration, and fear. My mom had some of all three, but I suspect she had a double measure of hurt and frustration. It's pretty hard, of course, to live around someone who wants to control you—and does—someone who is hypercritical, short on praise, and lives largely inside himself, as my dad did.

My mother suffered from a kind of anger I call "somatizing." It has to do with keeping your body in a constant state of readiness, but never using your physiological preparedness to do anything masterful to manage the sources of your hurt and frustration. When your adrenal glands pump adrenaline into your bloodstream, your body gets ready for action. If you never take the necessary action, you never reduce the pain. If the pain continues, you have to keep producing the adrenaline. Your body remains poised for too long. You develop some type of bodily breakdown. For my mother, it was constant headaches, digestive disturbances, and other forms of physical irritation. She was angry, you see, but she didn't have a ghost of an idea how to use her anger effectively—certainly not in her marriage with this good—but controlling—man.

My mother and father were married for more than seventy years, and in some ways it was a very good marriage. But they didn't experience much laughter and very little celebration. There was an absence of joy and delight, but an abundance of duty and obligation. It would have been a much better marriage if my mother could have used her anger more constructively.

Anger comes in many forms. Exploders often do terrible harm when they are angry. But somatizers like my mother are self-punishers, who take their anger out on their own self-concepts. Then there are the underhanders, who seldom take responsibility for their anger but try to place the anger in hurtful ways on others. Sarcasm, lack of punctuality, pouting, sexual acting out, and academic underachieving are examples of this underhanded anger.

But don't miss our text, one of the most unusual passages in all Scripture. It provides new insights into the management of anger. God himself becomes very angry with the children of Israel, and he threatens to wipe them out. He often becomes angry in the Bible. Of 455 times the word "anger" appears in the Old Testament, 375 of these refer to God's anger.

But, amazingly enough, in this text, Moses begged God to use his anger in a positive way. He reminded God of his promises and warned him of the terrible consequences if he acted aggressively on the basis of his blazing anger. God apparently listened to Moses, and we read, "Then the LORD relented and did not bring on his people the disaster he had threatened" (Exodus 32:14).

When you get angry, you can use it for positive outcomes. You don't need to be aggressive with it. In fact, you can use your heightened arousal to help you reach high and lofty goals. Anger can become one of your greatest allies. If you learn to manage your blazing inner state, you can make tremendous contributions to your marriage.

Lord Jesus, when we get angry with each other, help us to work for healing rather than for hurt. Teach us how to rehearse our purposes, how to use our arousal for good and not for evil. Thank you for giving us the power to deal with our pain. May we do so in ways that will bring honor and glory to our marriage and to your name. Amen.

The Union
of Two
Forgivers

Les and Leslie Parrott

Be kind and compassionate to one another, forgiving
each other, just as in Christ God forgave you.

EPHESIANS 4:32

Where's my suit you said you'd pick up from the cleaners?" asks the husband.

"I never said I'd get your suit."

"I can't believe you."

"Don't pass the blame to me; it's your suit."

"Yes, but I asked you last night to pick it up for me. Why didn't you?"

"You're crazy. We hardly even talked last night because you were at the game with Rick. Remember?"

"Oh, I get it. You didn't pick up my suit because you're mad about my going to the game."

"Wait a second, who's the one who gets mad if I'm not home to make dinner every night?"

This inane bleating goes on and on until, at last, one partner says, "I'm sorry. Will you forgive me?" In the daily grind of marriage, forgiveness keeps the relationship moving forward.

But for some agonizing couples, a devastating hurt calls on forgiveness to do much more than that. Betrayal can cut so deeply that forgiveness is the only cure that stands between a couple and their marriage's demise. It's their last hope to keep them from calling it quits. Can forgiveness bear that kind of weight? Is it fair to ask so much of it?

Yes, indeed. It is the very thing forgiveness was designed to do—to heal the deepest wounds of a human heart. Untold marriages have been saved by little more than forgiveness.

We all know couples who have suffered an unthinkable jolt and somehow, over time, made it through triumphantly. And when we ask those courageous couples how they did it, they eventually talk about forgiveness.

A marriage can't survive without it. Perhaps that's what spurred on Ruth Bell Graham to quip, "A happy marriage is the union of two good forgivers."

In addition to breaking the sick cycle of blame and loosening the death grip of guilt, forgiveness brings a couple together. Through forgiveness the offended spouse realizes he or she isn't as different from the wrongdoer as he or she would like to think. Surely this idea is what inspired Paul to write in Ephesians, "Be kind and compassionate to one another, forgiving each other, just as in Christ God forgave you."

Does forgiveness need to make a house call at your home? Have you both tried to ignore the hurts of your hearts at the peril of your relationship? Let forgiveness apply the healing salve of kindness and compassion to your wounds. And use these medicinal words: "I'm sorry. Will you forgive me?"

Lord, help us to bring forgiveness into our marriage. Show us how we can give grace to each other through the empowering forgiveness you give us. And help each of us not to become so caught up in our own hurt that we can't bring ourselves to be the first one to offer the kind, soft words of forgiveness.

EX-CU-U-SE
ME!

Neil Clark Warren

> He [Moses] said to Aaron, "What did these people do to you,
> that you led them into such great sin?" "Do not be angry,
> my lord," Aaron answered. "You know how prone these people
> are to evil. They said to me, 'Make us gods who will go
> before us'... So I told them, 'Whoever has any gold jewelry,
> take it off.' Then they gave me the gold, and I threw
> it into the fire, and out came this calf!"
>
> EXODUS 32:21–24

Marital excuse-making stands in the way of a lot of marriages
growing. I see it in my clinical practice almost every day.

I'll not soon forget the college professor who was as mad as
a hornet after the first session I spent with him and his wife.
When they got home, he said to her, "I'm *never* going to see that
psychologist again! I will not subject myself to that kind of cru-
elty. Count me out! Go by yourself if you want to, but don't even
think about my going with you. No more therapy for me!"

So, a few days later, when she came for the next session, she
told me what he had said. "I didn't even think about picking him

up for today's appointment," she told me, "because he made it clear he didn't want to be bothered." About halfway through our session, a loud knock sounded on my office door. Before I had a chance to open it, the middle-aged professor came blasting in. He was hot and perspiring, wearing a suit and carrying his brief-case. He had walked two miles from his campus to my office, and he was furious at his wife.

"Why didn't you pick me up?" he bellowed at her. "I waited and waited, but you never showed! What kind of a flake are you anyway?"

She was flabbergasted, but I gathered this wasn't the first time he had changed his mind without announcing his U-turn. "Well, Jim," she said softly but intensely, "you said over and over that you never wanted to come back to this office. You said you were through with therapy forever."

"I can't believe you took me seriously," the husband shouted with all the power his depleted state would allow. "You know I don't mean anything when I'm mad! Now listen to me," he said with his face about twelve inches from hers, "this is a perfect example of why we're not getting along. You don't have the good sense to take me seriously when I mean something and to forget what I say when I don't mean it! I just can't believe how stupid you are!"

Sometimes in a tight moment we become so irrational that we make outlandish statements in an effort to keep from being seen as irresponsible or immature. And we multiply our imma-turity and irresponsibility in that explosive moment.

One of the clearest biblical examples of this is the story of two brothers, Moses and Aaron. Moses went up to the mountain to meet with God and to receive the stone tablets that contained the Law. It was one of the biggest events in all of Jewish history.

When Moses didn't come back down the mountain right away, the people complained to Aaron that they needed a replacement leader. Aaron asked them to bring their gold earrings, and the Bible says that "Aaron melted the gold, then molded and tooled it into the form of a calf. The people exclaimed, 'O Israel, this is the god that brought you out of Egypt!'" (Exodus 32:4 LB).

When Moses came down from the mountain and saw the golden calf, his anger "burned." He asked Aaron, the trusted brother he had left in charge, "What did these people do to you, that you led them into such great sin?"

Now, here is one of the most pathetic, funny, irrational responses in the history of the human race. Aaron began rattling his jaws in an effort to keep himself from looking like the hollow, misdirected, sinful man he was. "Do not be angry," Aaron replied. Whenever someone tells you at a moment like this not to get so upset, get ready to be seriously upset. "You know how prone these people are to evil." Note that a person in trouble looks desperately for someone else to blame. "So I told them, 'Whoever has any gold jewelry, take it off.' Then they gave me the gold, and I threw it into the fire, and out came this calf!"

The penalty for Aaron's awful sin of leading the people to worship an idol was devastating. Under Moses' direction, three thousand people were killed by the Levites. More than that, Exodus 32:35 says, "And the LORD struck the people with a plague because of what they did with the calf Aaron had made."

When the truth isn't told in a marriage, when all kinds of lies, exaggerations, and irrational excuses are made, the result can be just as destructive to a marriage as Aaron's crazy behavior was destructive to Israel.

Sometimes the only right response in a situation is to be righteously upset—but it all depends on how right you are. If instead of being right, you are wrong, your "upset" can make you look silly for as long as anyone remembers your irrational display.

Dear Jesus, when we are in the wrong, help us to courageously admit it. Give us the kind of Christ-centered character that will allow us to tell each other the objective truth. Sometimes you know what a corner we find ourselves in. Teach us how to confess our stupidity and immaturity to each other in tough moments like those. And when we do, help us to forgive one another—to fume a little maybe—but to forgive. And, in time, help us to laugh with each other about our craziness. Even more, help us to learn and grow so that we don't end up with egg on our face so often. Amen.

IF YOU SAY THAT ONE MORE TIME . . .

Becky and Roger Tirabassi

> *Instead, speaking the truth in love, we will in all*
> *things grow up into him who is the Head, that is, Christ.*
>
> EPHESIANS 4:15

When Roger and I were first married, he could push one of my buttons that "sent me to the moon." When he said a certain phrase, I immediately would defend myself against his accusation. Now, I don't want to say he purposely used this phrase to hurt me, but it sure could send me into pandemonium. The phrase? "You're just like your mother."

Finally, during an unemotional, sane moment, we both concluded that this particular statement wasn't considered fair fighting. In fact, it had little to do with whatever problem was at hand and only served to create more anger and hurt. Thus we began to set rules for our disagreements that included barring certain statements. Each of us chose what statements we never wanted to hear again, and the mother comment was certainly one of mine!

Over time, we began to see conflict as a natural—or at least inevitable—part of married life. And we purposely focused on speaking the truth to each other *in love* . . . not in retaliation, meanness, or anger. We even began to concentrate on speaking in love when we communicated with our son and others.

Eventually, not only did it become a pattern in our lives, but Roger also developed Fourteen Rules for Communication that center around the concept of dousing your words with love.

Fourteen Rules for Effective Communication

1. Don't use the words "never" or "always."

2. Don't blame, shame, or use names.

3. Use "I" statements, rather than "you" statements.

4. Say "I am hurt" rather than "I am angry or mad."

5. Take a time-out if your emotions are getting out of control.

6. Don't withdraw or isolate.

7. Repeat back what the person said to you before you share your thoughts, feelings, and possible solutions.

8. Don't interrupt.

9. Don't demand.

10. Use the phrase "I would like . . ." rather than "I need."

11. Don't use threats.

12. Be affirming.

13. Never use, say, or ponder the "D" word ("divorce").

14. Don't use the phrase "You broke the rule."

Each rule is designed to teach a couple how to express their hurt rather than their anger and to avoid as much damage to the relationship as possible during those inescapable moments of conflict. Also, we need to acknowledge recurring anger issues, inherited traits, or other bad habits we have incorporated into our personalities since childhood, and we need to work to heal them as soon as possible.

In my case, Roger might have quit accusing me of being just like my mother, but I still had unresolved childhood issues that continued to cause outbursts of anger, unforgiveness, and bitterness. Intellectually, I knew that refusing to forgive and harboring unresolved anger wreaked havoc in my life, but it wasn't until I became accountable to a small group that I began to express my pain, admit my anger, and start to process those feelings.

As a result of much work, over time I began to heal in a very unexpected way. Now, if someone says to me, "You're just like your mother," I consider it a compliment! After all, my mother is a strong woman, helpful, athletic, a nurturer, and domestic, and she desires to grow spiritually daily.

Try to apply at least one of the fourteen communication principles to your marriage today. Maybe you could start by creating a list of off-limit statements. You'll find that your fighting will be fairer, your arguments will be resolved more quickly, and your feelings won't be as bruised. As an added and important benefit, you'll both "grow up into him who is the Head, that is Christ."

> Father, help us to communicate in loving ways with each other. Forgive us when we attack each other or lose our patience or self-control. Forgive us when we isolate and withdraw instead of communicating or praying together. Help us to avoid each other's hot buttons but instead help us to speak words that nurture and comfort. Amen.

SMILE, GRACIE

Nicole Johnson

*You turned my wailing into dancing; you removed
my sackcloth and clothed me with joy.*

PSALM 30:11

All the family members were standing in place, staring at the camera with silly grins waiting for the photographer to take the picture. We had gathered at our yearly celebration. The problem of the moment was my sister's youngest daughter, Gracie. She couldn't stay still. As hard as she tried, at the age of four, she found it far more interesting to stand on one foot than to firmly plant both of them and to pose for a picture. She was forced into place, and the scowl went all the way down to her toes.

"Stand still, Gracie."

She was one step away from tears.

"Smile, Gracie."

The corners of her mouth turned upward, but what formed on her lips wasn't a smile.

"Put your arms down by your side."

Arms thrust down.

135

"Now smile, please."

The same half-moon reappeared, this time going the wrong way.

"That isn't smiling, Gracie."

Tears flowed down her tiny cheeks. "How do I do that?"

We all laughed at the honesty of her question because we've all been there. The innocent beauty of young children surprises us because they're not skilled at wearing masks. While this honesty can be inconvenient for family photographs, it's refreshing. Children laugh when they are delighted, cry when they're sad, frown when they're puzzled, and scream when they're hurt. Unless they are taught otherwise.

Sadly, many of us were taught otherwise. I was. My parents divorced when I was six, and I was told to "smile." Like Gracie, I didn't know how to do that. Putting on a happy face was a contortion at best, a blatant deception at worst. And while I figured out how to turn up the corners of my mouth for the picture, I knew I wasn't smiling. The cost of pretending is high. The longer we do it, the more ingrained it becomes. It isolates us, keeping everyone from getting too close.

The higher our level of pretense, the farther we have to fall. We pretend in proportion to the fear of being found out. Many people bring tremendous pain into their marriages but are still showing up for their photographs smiling. Pretending blocks healing. Just showing up and smiling doesn't fix pain. If anything, it makes it worse. It keeps the tender subjects off limits and prevents us from getting to the bottom of what's wrong. Instead of working on the problems in our marriage, we simply try to smile like they aren't there. We hide the pain instead of investigating it. We never get to the bottom, where the real hurt is. And then we become a statistic. Everyone then wonders what happened to that couple who always seemed so happy.

Pretending that things are good when they aren't will not make them good. Working through the struggles we face is the only way to get to the other side.

Pretending gets old. That's why attending a church that encourages "the happy face" is the first thing to go when a couple begins to struggle. It's fine to attend worship services and Sunday school when things are going well, but when easy answers just won't work and your face is tired of smiling, that kind of church is the last place you want to be.

But a strong spiritual community really could be the best place for you, if you can allow a small group of people to handle the hard times with you. A church that will embrace you when you can't get your face to smile is a real church. A safe place like this is worth far more than gold when you need help sorting things out.

A real smile begins in the soul and then makes its way to your face. But when the soul isn't smiling, some investigating needs to be done. Rather than pasting on a half-moon smile and telling your feelings they don't matter, investigate what's wrong. Until you begin to understand, drop the mask and let a close friend (your spouse?) look with you. That person might see something you can't.

Jesus didn't come that we might be happy all the time; he came that we might have life. There is a difference. Life is full of bumps and bruises that hurt us but teach us, or challenge us and help us to grow. Happiness can be a relentless taskmaster that drives us toward Phoneyland. Christ doesn't demand a fake smile. He works from the inside on our lives. Our job, if you can call it that, is to let this relationship with him affect the outside of our lives, including our marriage. The key to not pretending is to bring our struggles to him, whether they be in our marriage or some other aspect of our lives. It's the best way to insure that

the next time the camera comes out, the smile on your face will
be a real one.

> *Father, thank you that we don't have to pose and act happy. You
> are big enough to handle our fears and hurts and kind enough
> to want to set us free from them. Thank you that your arms pro-
> vide a warm embrace and that when you reveal to us our weak-
> nesses and hurts, you don't startle us with a "flash" but treat us
> gently. Teach us how to be real with you and with each other.
> And most of all, may we let the work that you are doing in our
> souls make its way to our faces. Amen.*

THAT'S NONSENSE

Larry Crabb

Their words seemed to them like nonsense.

LUKE 24:11

I love you."
Yeah, right, we think to ourselves. *If you really loved me, you would . . .*, and the list is long.

Good words sometimes seem like nonsense—because they are. I remember a pastor sitting in my counseling office warmly declaring his deep love for his wife. She was unmoved. The words seemed hollow to me as well. I later discovered he was in the middle of his tenth affair.

But occasionally good words are true. The best words, the ones hardest to believe, are sometimes the truest words ever spoken. For example, "He's alive."

When the women returned from Christ's grave, having seen an angel who told them, "He isn't here. He is risen," they told the apostles. Luke records the apostles' response. "Their words seemed to them like nonsense."

Tell a man who has just discovered his wife is having an affair, "In even this, God is working toward something good, something so good that you'll one day be grateful for the path that got you there," and the words will seem like nonsense.

Tell a busy mom packing up four kids to take them to four different places, "In everything give thanks and God's peace will calm your heart. You can rest by still water," and she'll probably scream. Maybe she'll whack you. "Rest? I can rest? Suppose you take my kids for two weeks and buy me a plane ticket to Hawaii. Then I can rest."

Probably the words that seem most like nonsense to me are Jesus' words, "Be of good cheer; I have overcome the world" (John 16:33 KJV).

Be of good cheer? A close relative has just died. My mother has Alzheimer's. My mother-in-law had a heart attack last week. I spent yesterday afternoon in bed with a headache that my medicine didn't touch. Ten projects are pressing for completion, and all my friends think they're busier than I am. Cheer? Maybe I should lift a glass with anesthetizing liquid in it and say, "Cheers." *That* makes sense.

No, it doesn't. But Jesus' words do. He *is* alive. He *does* care. If he walked up to me right now, he would say, "I am so glad to see you. I'm delighted to have you for a friend. Stick close to me. Where we're headed is fantastic! You'll love it. Hang on! Hold my hand."

A friend recently told me he felt pain so intense he considered ending his life. Words about cheer, hope, and joy seemed like nonsense to him.

But they're not! Soon the best news will be undeniably real. Till then, follow Jesus. Love your spouse. Be good to your family. God's Word is true.

Dear Lord, we don't see very well. The clouds seem so often to block out the sunshine. You've told us you have everything under control. You've invited us to rest. We confess that what you say sometimes seems like nonsense. It just doesn't feel true. Help us to believe anyway, to know that whatever you say is true. Help us to rest in your wonderful Word.

When the Honeymoon Is Over

Gary Smalley

> *A gentle answer turns away wrath, but*
> *a harsh word stirs up anger.*
>
> PROVERBS 15:1

After twenty-five years of being single, Sandy was about to marry the man of her dreams. She had been dating Larry for four years and thought she knew him inside out. Their courtship had its ups and downs, but all things considered, she knew their love was so strong that living happily ever after would be as natural as waking up in the morning.

The wedding day finally came, and it was everything she had dreamed about. Larry really was Prince Charming.

Then came the honeymoon. And she began to see a side of Larry she hadn't known existed. On the fourth day of the honeymoon, Larry decided Sandy would enjoy seeing where he used to work in the summers during college. So they began their five-mile hike at an eight-thousand-foot elevation in the High Sierras (something every woman dreams of doing on the fourth day of her honeymoon). By the time they arrived at their destination, she was exhausted. Since they had to be back at the lodge by dark, they had time for only a short rest.

Later, when they reached the lodge, she had a new concept of physical exhaustion. Prince Charming was tired too so they immediately went to bed. (Actually, he leaped, and she crawled.) To her amazement, the Prince didn't want to sleep—he had more exciting things in mind. From that point on, disappointment became the hallmark of her life.

She had entered marriage thinking Larry would dedicate himself to meeting her needs. After all, he had said in his wedding vows that he would love and cherish her for better or for worse, for richer or for poorer, in sickness and in health, until death. In his particular vows, which he had written, he even had said he committed himself to provide for all her needs for the rest of his life. But the vows were quickly becoming mere ceremonial words, and her needs obviously were secondary to his.

She thought she could change him by demanding in various ways that he become more considerate. After eight years, things had only become worse. She finally resigned herself to accept that her relationship with Larry never would improve.

Larry, of course, was convinced the marriage problems were Sandy's fault. He thought of her as demanding and argumentative. She no longer respected or appreciated him as she had when they were dating.

But then, an amazing thing happened. Now Larry is no longer the self-centered, inconsiderate, demanding husband he was. Sandy's eyes sparkle when she talks about the ways he daily shows his love for her, how he considers her desires even above his own needs. He has become the sensitive husband she always dreamed about. He provides all the strength she'll ever need and yet loves her with gentleness and care.

What happened? Sandy began to use two principles whenever she approached Larry about his insensitivity to her.

No one likes to be criticized, regardless how much truth lies behind the criticism. Whether we are male or female, six or sixty, when someone corrects us, we automatically become defensive. Yet honest communication is vital to marriage. These two basic truths appear contradictory. How do you honestly tell the one you love about something you find displeasing or aggravating without prompting that familiar, defensive glare or indifferent shrug?

First, learn to express your feelings with warmth, empathy, and sincerity. Warmth is expressed by communicating a friendly acceptance of the other person. Empathy is the ability to understand and identify with a person's feelings. And sincerity involves being genuinely concerned about a person.

Second, learn to wait until your anger or feelings of irritability have subsided before discussing a sensitive issue—and then talk about how you feel rather than how the other person should behave.

These two principles allow your mate to receive your comments and leave room for him or her to change. It won't happen like waving a magic wand or saying three enchanting words that render the other person into the individual you *thought* you were marrying. But slowly and surely, these principles open the door for a very different kind of magic—the power of love—to rekindle your relationship.

Lord, help me express myself in such a way that my spouse knows deeply of my love and admiration. Enable both of us to say what we feel but to do it in a way that encourages change rather than stubbornness, that brings renewal rather than retreat to our relationship. Thank you that love has the power to make us more of who we can be.

Part Six

Celebrating Our Future Together

Hand
in Hand

Becky and Roger Tirabassi

*In the morning I lay my requests before
you and wait in expectation.*

PSALM 5:3

When Roger and I decided I should travel and speak full-time, we also decided Roger would be the "at-home" parent and leave his full-time job for a part-time one. While we were making these decisions, we also were praying and asking God if we should move and if Roger should consider a career change.

We had been living in California for only five years and didn't really want to leave the area, but Roger felt we should explore a number of options. So we put a few feelers out with friends in other occupations and inquired about job openings.

Three options surfaced:

1. A job in a college on the East Coast. The pay would be comparable, the duties intellectually challenging, but the

weather would return us to the freezing cold winters that we had so happily left behind.

2. A job in another county in California, which would cause us to move. The position was part-time, and Roger would train and mentor youth workers, but the job description included raising our own salary rather than having it provided.

3. A part-time position as a youth pastor at a church only one mile from our house. This job included the development of a Twelve-Step program for students, and the salary was the best of the three offers.

In my mind, the third option was the best, easiest, and most preferred. I considered this decision a no-brainer, but Roger felt we needed to ask the Lord to show us clearly which job was right for us.

I thought of this as a risky prayer, but we had always made prayer an integral part of our decision-making process, especially when it affected our marriage. Whenever we sold a house or bought a car, we would ask God to give both of us a "green light" and an inner confidence about the final decision. We felt that was the best way to maintain a sense of oneness between each other and God—and to be assured this was the direction God was leading.

This time, because we both didn't have the same definitive nudge, we decided to ask God to close the doors to the jobs that weren't right for us and to leave open only one opportunity. We prayed daily about each of the job opportunities, and we watched and waited to see what God would do.

In less than a week the college called to inform us that the new teaching position was going to be put on hold, as the school waited one more year before adding funds to the program. Shortly after that, a call came regarding the youth worker position. The board of that organization had decided not to add more staff to its budget, and that job also was being placed on hold. But the offer to develop a program for hurting teens in the local church remained "on the table" with enthusiastic and strong support from all of the parties.

We had laid our requests before God and waited in expectation, as Psalm 5 says, and we were thrilled by the way it all worked out. But equally thrilling, deep in our hearts, was being convinced the job we had wanted was also the job God had wanted for us. The process of seeking the Lord together and waiting to see how he would respond drew Roger and me closer, making us more aware of our oneness before God and the connectedness he had intended for us to have, even in the process of making some hard decisions.

When several paths await you and you wonder what to do, hold one another's hand and seek God. He'll show you what to do, and the two of you can move forward, hand in hand, just the way it was intended to be.

> *Lord, help us always to bring our requests to you, being patient to wait on you as you orchestrate events and circumstances. Remind us not to let go of each other's hand as we pray and wait, that this is something we do as a couple. Help us to maintain our faith and trust in you. Thank you for hearing us and for the assurance that your will is best—and will be done. Amen.*

NEVER, NEVER, NEVER

Larry Crabb

> *May the LORD make the woman who is coming into your home like Rachel and Leah, who together built up the house of Israel.*
>
> RUTH 4:11

Have you ever reached a point in your marriage where you felt you just couldn't continue? More couples than you might suspect have been there. Look at that older couple who enjoy being together, the ones with the marriage you would love to have. Chances are they came close to calling it quits at least once, maybe more.

Sometimes the obstacles seem too great: infidelity, name calling, coldness that rivals the South Pole, and differences and tensions that lead only to impasses.

If you've ever been there—or when it happens—dust off a book of England's recent history and read the shortest, greatest speech ever made to a graduating class of college students. Winston Churchill walked to the podium, looked at the rows of idealistic faces that anticipated nothing but realized dreams and smooth sailing, and with the wisdom of age said to those young innocents, "Never, never, never, never, never, never, never, never, NEVER GIVE UP!" Then he returned to his seat and sat down.

But why shouldn't we quit? Doesn't it sometimes make good sense just to accept defeat?

Quitting is declaring that God isn't quite up to the job of cooking up something good out of the mess you're in. But that's not true. Never, never, never!

The most celebrated marriage in the Old Testament was the union of Ruth and Boaz. (Read the book of Ruth; it will take you less than half an hour.) What stands out to me about that wedding is the toast offered by Boaz's best man at the rehearsal dinner.

While the glasses tinkled, the best man rose to his feet, smiled at Boaz, and said, "May the LORD make the woman who is coming into your home like Rachel and Leah, who together built up the house of Israel" (Ruth 4:11).

At first glance, that toast makes little sense. If you know your Bible, it makes even less sense.

Let me remind you of a slice of Jewish history. Leah was the unattractive woman, the one Jacob didn't want, whom her father pawned off on Jacob. Rachel, Jacob's second wife, was the pretty one who couldn't have kids and was furious that Leah could.

After Leah gave birth to four sons by Jacob (each time hoping Jacob would finally love her), Rachel told Jacob to sleep with her maid. He did and had two sons by her. Then Leah couldn't get pregnant again so she offered her maid to Jacob. The result? Two more sons.

Then Leah conceived, twice. Now Jacob had ten sons. He kept sleeping with Rachel—she was good looking—and surprisingly she had her first son, Joseph. Then she gave birth to Benjamin and died in the process, naming him *Son of My Trouble* (Jacob renamed him *Son of My Strength.*)

That's the story of how the twelve sons of Jacob (whom God renamed Israel) arrived on the scene to begin the nation through whom the Messiah would come. The twelve tribes of Israel began through two neurotic women.

"May your wife be like Rachel and Leah." What did the best man mean? May Ruth be insecure? A competitive schemer? An end-justifies-the-means kind of woman?

Let me tell you what I hear in that toast: The failure of people never defeats the purposes of God. Hang in there. After all, we're saved today because God worked through a very dysfunctional family to send Jesus to Earth.

Lift your eyes to see the unseen world. Right now, exactly where you are in your marriage, whether celebrating the wonder of it or wondering why you ever thought about celebrating it, God is at work. Something good—or even better—is on its way. Never, never, NEVER GIVE UP!

Dear Lord, we won't weigh anchor on our marriage. Even when discouragement hits us with more force than a gale wind. Even when we betray one another through small deeds or big ones. Even when we feel as though we would do anything to be released from the pain. But, Lord, we recognize that we'll be able to stay the course only if you strengthen us, only if you enable us to find forgiveness and tenderness when those attributes have rushed out the door with the wind. We look to you for grace, for peace, for mercy, and for love. May we, failed people like Rachel and Leah, be used by you.

THE CAROUSEL

Nicole Johnson

Anyone who listens to the word but does not do what it says is like a man who looks at his face in a mirror and, after looking at himself, goes away and immediately forgets what he looks like.

JAMES 1:23–24

We were in Hampton, Virginia, walking near our hotel when we saw an outdoor pavilion that housed an old-fashioned carousel. We both smiled and made our way toward the entrance. The place was just about to close for the evening, but we plunked down a buck for us both and picked our horses for the last ride. Paul chose a cream stallion that leaped and lurched under a multi-colored saddle. I selected a black beauty with fire in his eyes and a red saddle on his back. We were the only ones on the carousel that warm, muggy Southern night, and as the music blared and we went round and round, we entered a magical, romantic world of painted landscapes and mirrored lights. We could have ridden forever.

Then the music stopped, and the horses came to a standstill. The magic ended, and we were ushered off the ride. Just like that. Illusion was stripped away, and we were back on the street again, walking the pavement in silence. No lights, no glitter, no motion.

My life can be like that carousel. I am drawn in by the music and lights, and I pick a horse that I think will take me somewhere enchanting. I laugh and enjoy the ride, never thinking about how I'm passing the same things over and over. I don't hear that the music is canned, notice that the scenery is painted, or see that the people around me aren't going anywhere either. Until something breaks the illusion.

Please don't misunderstand. Carousels are wonderful rides for children and fun experiences for adults, but too many of us never get off the blasted thing. We continue the illusion of actually going somewhere or doing something significant while we're spinning around a painted destination.

But contrast those fiberglass stallions with the real thing, replace those painted landscapes with a living sunrise, and you'll be glad you're off.

Each of us was created with a mission and a purpose that was placed in us before the world's foundation. But we get distracted. We buy a ticket to the carousel and spend the next twenty years on it. A job that begins with glamour can keep us circling forever. Raising a family can become a carousel in no time, and even our marriages, if we aren't careful, can turn into a not so merry go-round.

Find your mission. Define your purpose. That helps you to recognize circles. Pay attention and stay alert. When you start to feel that you've seen the landscape before, been there a hundred times, done that forever, you're probably on a carousel. Write a mission statement for your life and for your marriage. It's the only way to know if you're moving forward rather than repeating the same old same old.

Antoine de Saint-Exupery wrote, "Love does not consist in gazing at each other, but in looking together in the same direction." Set that direction like a mark on the horizon and find the living horses that can carry you there.

> Holy Spirit, show us how to tell the real from the illusory. Show us the carousels in our lives that keep us from doing something significant by distracting us with glitter, lights, and mirrors. Give us the power to step off and begin real life, filled with the passion and purpose that you have placed in our hearts. Amen.

This Is Dedicated to the One I Love

Les and Leslie Parrott

Know therefore that the LORD your God is God;
he is the faithful God, keeping his covenant of love to a
thousand generations of those who love him
and keep his commands.

DEUTERONOMY 7:9

For better or for worse, for richer or for poorer, in sickness and in health, until death do us part." Just words. Mere phrases, really. You hear them at every wedding. Are you impressed? Probably not. It's one thing to say those words; it's another to keep them. Let's face it, it's a covenant that bears out only over the course of a lifetime. And half the time it doesn't.

Bill Lake, a 103-year-old married man in Yakima, Washington, has proved his pledge. He does so unfailingly every day, sitting next to Gladys in the convalescent center, watching her body slowly shut down from the ravages of Parkinson's disease. Her hands once shook with the disease, but now they have gone still. Her speech in healthier times was fluid, but she now is mute. Her face, which used to light up at seeing her husband, now is frozen.

"It isn't very pleasant for me or her," Bill says. "But what can you do?" What Bill does is pure dedication. He sits in the chair next to Gladys's bed for four hours a day, a visit in the morning and another in the afternoon. He passes the time reading to her, talking out their life together or simply sitting—making good on the promise he made seventy-two years ago.

When he arrives for each of his visits, Bill brushes back Gladys's silver hair and greets her with a kiss on the head and a soothing voice. "Hi, sweetie. Can you hear me?" Her eyes just roll.

For better or for worse. You'd better believe it. Bill has been visiting his wife in the convalescent center for nearly ten years. In that time he's seen people drop off relatives and never return. He's seen people die lonely. But he promises that won't happen to his wife while he's alive. We have a strong feeling he's right.

"Till death do us part" is not an ideal. It is a reality that is insured by an unswerving commitment—a willful agreement to keep love alive. "Do two walk together unless they have agreed to do so?" asked the prophet Amos (3:3). Commitment is the cerebral part of love. It's the part that comes more from our minds than our hearts.

Why do so many marriage commitments fall flat these days? We believe it's because too many promises are made without the promises of God. We can "hold unswervingly to the hope we profess, for he who promised is faithful" (Hebrews 10:23). Our commitment to each other in marriage is sustained by God's model of faithfulness to us. When a man and woman covenant with one another, God promises faithfulness to them (see 1 Corinthians 1:9). We can't overemphasize the centrality of commitment in God's character. It's woven into every part of the

Bible—from Genesis, where God initiates his promise of faithfulness, through Revelation, where John's vision depicts "a white horse, whose rider is called Faithful and True" (19:11).

The commitment we made and accepted in marriage enfolds our whole soul by saying, "I believe in you and commit myself to you through thick and thin." Without commitment and the trust it engenders, marriage would have no hope of enduring. But no couple can achieve deep confidence in the fidelity of themselves and each other until they first recognize God's faithfulness to them.

"For better or for worse, for richer or poorer, in sickness and in health, until death do us part." Just words? Mere phrases? Not when they envelop a love relationship that spans months, years, decades. Or in Bill Lake's case, almost three-quarters of a century.

Father, the inspiration that comes from couples who have kept their commitment for so many years is a true blessing. Help us to learn from couples who have lived out their wedding vows. Help us to bring the too-often lofty ideal of commitment down to the daily reality of our lives. And remind us that it is only by your strength that we could ever keep our promise to love until death. Fill our marriage with the strength of your covenant. Amen.

WHAT PART
OF 5:30 a.m.
DON'T YOU LIKE?

Gary Smalley

*A fool gives full vent to his anger, but a wise
man keeps himself under control.*

PROVERBS 29:11

Do you ever wonder what truly causes divorce? Believe it or
not, researchers have discovered that couples who divorce
basically become infected with at least one of the four divorce
germs. Couples stay in love for hundreds of positive reasons, but
only four root problems cause divorce. Before I tell you about
the four germs, let me share how I managed to infect my marriage with all four of them in the span of one hour, which is no
small feat.

Every year Norma and I try to plan a seminar located in a
vacation spot. This particuiar year it was Hawaii. We were staying at a beautiful hotel on Diamond Bay; the scene from our balcony was breathtaking. The morning before the seminar I was
on the balcony admiring the sun as it rose over Hilton Head.
The light rays danced across the ocean surface, reminding me

how precious life is and how lucky I am to have such a great wife
and family.

Norma was still sleeping. She had told me she wanted to
sleep in that morning because she was tired. But I couldn't imagine that she would want to miss God's glory just to catch up on
some sleep. Besides, I was inspired to work on our marriage goals
for the upcoming year, and this would be the perfect opportunity. Oh, did I mention it was 5:30?

So I crept into the room and gently tapped Norma's shoulder. She rolled over. I didn't let that discourage me. As I tugged
at the covers, she sat up and asked what time it was. I said, "It's
5:30. Why?"

"Why? Because I told you I wanted to sleep in till eight. Now
leave me alone."

In my mind, Norma didn't really mean she wanted to be left
alone; so I ripped off the covers, hoping that my playfulness
might warm her up to the idea of getting out of bed.

We ended up having a discussion, all right, but it wasn't
about our marriage goals. Norma threw some zingers my way so
I raised her a few zingers, and before we knew it, we had inhaled
more than our share of the four divorce germs.

What are the four germs? Escalation. Withdrawal. Name calling. And negative beliefs.

When an argument spirals out of control, and you both say
things you don't mean, you've experienced escalation. Withdrawal involves avoiding arguments completely by either not
talking or leaving the premises. Name calling, or devaluing your
mate, is when you criticize and say things to put down your
spouse. The last germ, negative beliefs, involves believing your
mate is trying to ruin your marriage.

Men frequently are accused of having contracted this last germ. But I want to dispel that theory. Please understand that men don't try to ruin their marriages; it just comes naturally.

The moral of my story is that it's easy to be infected with the four divorce germs. Even a guy who has given marriage advice for more than thirty years still gets exposed to them. The important thing is to learn to recognize when your marriage is infected. Then you need to do just what you would do if you had the flu: pay attention to your illness, address the problems straight on, and give yourselves some quiet time. *Enjoy* being together instead of fighting or withdrawing. Concentrate on drawing each other out and recalling what it was you loved about each other all along.

It's inevitable you'll be exposed to the four divorce germs several times in your years together. But to have a bright future, be sure not only to try to avoid the germs but also to liberally apply the remedies. That's the best way to assure a healthy future for your partnership. Oh, and don't wake your spouse up at 5:30 in the morning to plan that future—it just might bug your mate.

Lord, give each of us a humble spirit that enables us to listen to that little voice you have placed in our souls, the one that tells us how to love each other to the fullest. Then remind us of the ways in which love has sustained and blessed us in the past and help us to find that love all over again. Renew and replenish our supply of love; inoculate us against the germs that can destroy what we've worked so hard to build. Amen.

Dream a Little Dream of Us

Neil Clark Warren

> *"In my dreams I also saw seven heads of grain, full*
> *and good, growing on a single stalk. After them, seven*
> *other heads sprouted—withered and thin and scorched by*
> *the east wind. The thin heads of grain swallowed up the seven good*
> *heads. I told this to the magicians, but none could explain it to me."*

GENESIS 41:22–24

Few statements that I could make would produce the kind of attentiveness this one does: "Let me tell you what your dream means."

I've been a practicing clinical psychologist for thirty-five years, and I've heard thousands of people tell me their dreams in hopes of discovering their inner secrets. I've given my best shot at interpreting hundreds of these dreams, and some of my interpretations struck me, and my clients I think, as unusually creative. Most of my creations took dream interpretation theory into consideration. If pressed, I could have made at least a weak argument on behalf of my concoctions.

But, in reality, I don't have any confidence in my ability to interpret dreams. People keep wanting to put confidence in me, but I assure them that such a belief is resting on a shaky foundation. I have no confidence in other current dream interpreters either. I've read some books, attended some meetings, and finally concluded that most dream interpretation has about the same accuracy as efforts at extrasensory perception. Under careful examination, the accuracy is low and the wisdom is superficial.

But I think a certain kind of dreaming has enormous value. What a difference it makes when lovers dream together about their marriage! Too often people wander into marriage with an inadequate dream. They become easy targets for disappointment, temptation, conflict, boredom, and confusion.

Marylyn and I have done a lot of dreaming through the forty years of our marriage. Some of it has been wonderful, but I'm ashamed of the early dreaming we did. Granted, it was a number of years ago, but we have no excuse for how heavily we emphasized my career and my life, often at the expense of our life together. Somehow, the dream for her life was supposed to be a part of my life. We focused too little on those parts that would provide deep satisfaction for her needs.

Fortunately, we have corrected this glaring error in our marriage. I now know that if this oversight remains unchanged in a marriage, one or both partners will suffer.

We keep our marital dreams up-to-date. Now that our three daughters are married, we have a different dream for our marriage than we had ten or fifteen years ago.

And we constantly ask ourselves if our dream is broad enough. For instance, we're eager to develop our spiritual sides as well as our physical and economic sides.

That's where our efforts with Couples of Faith have proven so crucial. Marylyn takes off work to attend every event with me. We listen to the other speakers, whom we have heard many times. Something new always comes to us. And when Wayne Watson sings at these events, he inspires both of us in powerful ways.

Marylyn and I find that dreaming together is very romantic. We actually think that dreaming and envisioning our life are the essence of our romance. We're convinced that any couple who dreams about their future together is bound to fall in love over and over and over. Nothing in the world is as attractive as someone who will dream with you, merge their dreams with yours, clarify the path toward the realization of those dreams, and lock their arms into yours while walking down the path.

At the center of all this dreaming and planning is a constantly recurring theme: "I want the future to be good for you. If it isn't good for you, it can't be good for us. Whatever is good and healthy for you, we'll find a way to make it work in our life together."

Do you hear that theme? I want it to be good for *you*. Being cared for this way is at the core of romance.

We've been married for a long time, and I've listened to thousands of couples in my practice. I know that if the two of you keep your marital dream alive and vital, it will fill your marriage with energy. It will set you free to know the joy that comes from moving forward through life with the person you love more than any other. When you work out your marital dreams, you can glide—for the two of you will be merged and bonded, and your hearts will be welded together forever.

Dear Father, you are the one who has called us together. You are the one whose Spirit gives us life and power. Help us to dream a dream for our marriage that has your Spirit at the center. And when we do, help us to stay alert to our joy. In the name of your Son. Amen.

Part Seven
Celebrating Each
Other's Gifts

The Leman Checkbook Checks Out

Dr. Kevin Leman

There are different kinds of gifts, but the same Spirit.
There are different kinds of service, but the
same Lord. There are different kinds of working, but
the same God works all of them in all men.

1 CORINTHIANS 12:4–6

At our house, we decided long ago that it would be better if Sande took care of the checkbook. Things just "balance" better when she does, if you know what I mean. She does a great job keeping track of things, no thanks to me.

Having grown up as the lastborn of my family, I didn't develop that fine appreciation for order and sequence. I'm working at it because I know it's a weakness, but I'm not equipped with natural ability and preference to handle the checkbook.

I'm always amazed when, once a month, the bank sends us a detailed list of the checks we've written, and they even include the number of the checks. My response is, "What's all this for?" But Sande pounces on the bank statement like a cat on a mouse. I guess she's afraid I'll mistake it for junk mail.

Turning the checkbook and bill paying over to Sande was a *partial* answer to our problem. But it was just too much trouble for me to carry around my own separate checkbook, so I made it a habit to tear out a check or two from her checkbook and put them in my wallet for emergencies. Then, when I had to write a check, I would just go ahead and do so. But usually I would forget to record what I wrote. Later, when Sande tried to balance the checkbook with that once-a-month statement from the bank, she had to wrestle with check numbers that were out of sequence or checks that hadn't been returned because they were still in my wallet.

After some fairly serious "unbalanced checkbook sessions," I decided to make a real effort to reform. Now I take blank checks only from Sande's checkbook, not from the supply in her drawer, and when I write a check, I really try to remember to give her a note with a check number and the amount.

I confess this little weakness of mine to point out that it would be silly for us to leave me in charge of the checkbook. Sande, who seems naturally born to checkbook balancing, is the gifted one. And I gladly defer to her.

You might be surprised at ways you as a couple have been limping along because one of you isn't particularly apt at a function generally considered that sex's strong suit. It always does my heart good to see a couple willing to go outside convention's boundaries and to express their gifts in ways that work. For example, one couple found the wife should be the "handyman" around the house. And she liked to use the push lawnmower. Any power source besides her muscle was considered powder-puff stuff to her. The husband was the family chef. She wanted power tools for Christmas; he'd be happy with a new food processor.

Reassigning responsibilities according to giftedness starts with sitting down and talking about who is doing what and why. You both will undoubtedly learn something—and strengthen your marriage in the process.

Father, teach us to celebrate one another's gifts, to appreciate what each of us brings to our union, making us a whole that functions better than the two halves separately. Help us to bear with one another's weaknesses and not to be resentful of the other's strengths. Amen.

WINNING ISN'T EVERYTHING

Neil Clark Warren

> *Peter asked Jesus, "What about him [John], Lord?*
> *What sort of death will he die?" Jesus replied,*
> *"If I want him to live until I return, what is*
> *that to you? You follow me."*

JOHN 21:21—22 LB

*C*omparisons in marriage have zero potential for marital gain! Nevertheless, my wife, Marylyn, and I fall prey to them every once in a while.

Of course, just for comparison's sake, I have to say I'm sure she starts the ugly process more than I do. It works like this: She comes home from work and cooks dinner, placing it on the table as I return from a long day. When we finish eating, she assumes I will clean up everything.

Wait! I think. *I started my day earlier, I am in a much more demanding profession, and I shouldn't have to confront this mass of dirty dishes and counters.*

Hold on, mister! she thinks. *My work is just as hard as yours, and I prepared the whole dinner. That requires ten times more energy than just cleaning up the dishes.*

Mind you, we carry on this comparison of burdens without ever saying a word. After forty years of marriage, words become unnecessary.

If Marylyn and I let ourselves, we could spend most of our time comparing. She is a lot better looking than I am, but I earn substantially more than she does. She accepts many more responsibilities around our home than I do, but I study and pray more than she does. Our three married daughters adore Marylyn, and they all talk frequently with each other, but I . . . well, you get the idea. Comparisons in marriage are endless.

But they do no good! And they lead to the wrong dynamic. Instead of increasing marital love, they steadily subtract from it. The real secret is to knock ourselves out serving one another instead of struggling to gain superiority.

The apostle Peter, I'm convinced, had a habit of comparing himself with the other disciples. Jesus saw Peter as a potentially powerful leader, but his impulsiveness kept sabotaging his good intentions. And his impulsiveness, I suspect, was motivated by his eagerness to "please the teacher," to win points, to move to the head of the class. He made bigger boasts than anyone else, but try as hard as he could, he seldom backed his boasts with the behavior he promised.

The disciple John, also an apostle, frequently bettered Peter when comparisons became the focus. My friend Dr. Dale Bruner, an insightful Bible teacher, pointed out to me recently that "the beloved disciple," a title which tradition assigns to John, is mentioned in the last half of John's gospel seven times. Five of those times, the beloved disciple and Peter are mentioned together (implying comparison). John generally came out on top. At the end of the book, after Jesus has asked Peter three times if he loved Jesus, Jesus tells Peter how he is going to die. Jesus concludes the encounter by simply instructing Peter to "follow me."

Peter prepares to move away, but he turns around and sees John already following Jesus. The unrelenting comparison puts Peter in a negative light one more time. His competitive instinct eats him up. His frustration takes over, and he blurts out a pointed question to Jesus: "What about him, Lord? What sort of death will he die?"

Jesus may or may not have raised his voice a little, but he certainly made it clear that he was frustrated by Peter's jealousy, born of his need to compare. "If I want him to live until I return, what is that to you? You follow me." Jesus was saying, "Peter, what happens to John is not your business. Your whole focus should revolve around following me."

So, how are you doing in your effort to stop making comparisons in your marriage? I keep trying, but I need regular reminders. I get so frustrated when Marylyn reads three books to my one, gets ready for bed twice as fast as I do, understands jokes that I don't get, and generally outshines me in a score of comparison games.

I need to keep remembering that "winning" isn't the secret to a great marriage. God's love for me makes my value secure, and Marylyn's love for me will multiply when I celebrate her gifts instead of competing with them.

So here's how I'm trying to handle my addiction to comparisons. I remind myself over and over that Jesus loves Marylyn and me exactly the same, that the two of us are on the same team, that every time she does something wonderful, we both profit from it, and that this matter of "one flesh" makes it crucial for *both* of us to do our best for the marriage and family of which we are a part.

But I have to tell you, Marylyn is taking it easy this Saturday morning, and I'm sitting here working my head off!

> *Dear Jesus, we confess that sometimes we think of your love as the prize for being better, working harder, or being right. Help us to remember that you totally love both of us, that our worth is never at risk because of anything between us. Give us the generosity of spirit that makes us pull hard for each other under every circumstance. And may we never lose sight of how much you want us to love each other the way you loved the church when you died for it. Amen.*

STRONGER TOGETHER

Becky and Roger Tirabassi

> *Your word is a lamp to my feet and a light for*
> *my path. . . . I rise before dawn and cry for help;*
> *I have put my hope in your word.*
>
> PSALM 119:105, 147

Before I met Roger, he had attended a seminar, along with busloads of other people from all over Cleveland, in which the speaker encouraged and challenged the attendees to commit to read the Bible at least five minutes a day. Roger made that decision in 1973—and has kept it.

After I met Roger in 1976, he told me of his daily Bible reading and encouraged me to make the same commitment. I took the plunge.

But by the early 1980s, I had wavered. I still was convinced daily Bible reading was a good idea and should be a high priority; I just couldn't seem to make it a habit. I had great intentions, but I either fell asleep while reading my Bible or continually put off reading it until I had forgotten to do it.

Even though I was a youth worker, Bible reading and even prayer had turned into more of a duty than an opportunity to spend time with the living, loving God. Then, one winter morning in 1984, I found myself "going through the motions" of leading a Bible study for eight varsity cheerleaders whom I coached at the local high school. During this particular breakfast meeting at Bob's Big Boy restaurant, I began to give specific instructions on how to make Bible reading and prayer a daily habit. In the middle of teaching, I thought, *Becky, you don't even do this, yet you expect these high school girls to do it?* I pushed away the thought and wrapped up our time together.

A few weeks later, I found myself at a convention in Chicago. I was surprised to hear all the speakers talk passionately about the Word and prayer. As if awakened to the truth about "time with God," I was electrified with the thought of actually having an "appointment with the King." At that convention, I discovered prayer as Rosalind Rinker expressed it: "A conversation between two people who love each other." For the first time I understood that prayer was more than a monologue but a two-way conversation.

Roger's commitment to listen to God daily by reading the Bible and by talking to God daily in writing (or journaling) was a strength he brought to our relationship. His ability to see the benefits of such a discipline touched my life deeply and has become the focus of our ministry. We also believe that commitment has strengthened our marriage. It has prodded us individually to seek God and to hear his voice, to be open to seeing ourselves in new ways and to growing. As we fall more deeply in love with God, it gives us so much more to bring into our marriage.

I'm thankful Roger paved the way with his strong commitment and faithfulness so I, who lacked the discipline he seemed to have in abundance, could follow him on that path.

Because of the blessings we've seen from this habit, we encourage every couple to make a lifelong decision to spend at least ten minutes a day in the Word and prayer. Why don't you discuss—maybe even right now—how you can grow together spiritually?

Lord, please help us to remember that your Word lights our path; that it gives us direction, correction, and protection. We need and want to communicate with you on a daily basis. Please help us to open our Bibles, and cause us to hear your voice. Help us each to pour our hearts out to you in prayer like children. Cause us to know you better and love you more every day. Amen.

When North and South Converge

Dr. Kevin Leman

But [God] said to me, "My grace is sufficient for you,
for my power is made perfect in weakness."

2 CORINTHIANS 12:9

A friend of mine once confided in me that, when he became engaged, he was told marriage would bring out his weaknesses. Wanting to be prepared, he asked, "Which ones?"

"All of them," he was told.

The wonderful—and painful—thing about marriage is that God matches us up in such a way that one's strengths are often the other's weaknesses. And, as you live together, God pulls you both in from opposite poles to meet in the middle. It's as if he moves you in a bit from the frozen North and your mate in from the tropical South.

For example, differences between you and your spouse come into play in a hurry when the children start to arrive. How were you and your spouse parented? How do each of you see the parenting task? If the husband was raised by authoritarian parents, he might want to be authoritarian as well. On the other hand, he could be so fed up with the "you'd better toe the mark" approach that he'll want to go completely permissive as his personal vendetta against his authoritarian upbringing.

For the sake of illustration, suppose the husband wants to be authoritarian, but his wife, who was raised by permissive parents, much prefers the laissez-faire approach to dealing with her kids. Every time he moves in to do some disciplining, she moves in to protect them. With piranhalike instincts, kids sense these inconsistencies in a flash, and they quickly learn how to pit one parent against the other while trying to avoid being disciplined.

One day on the radio program I cohost, our subject was getting kids to cooperate at home. Our guests were Charlene and Dan, parents of a blended family who had grappled with this problem of learning how to work together in disciplining the children.

Dan was the quiet, passive type who hated hassles and preferred to avoid trouble whenever possible. Charlene had been reared in a military family, and she had taken over the role of disciplinarian. Dan had allowed her to do so, and he often would "escape" by leaving the dinner table or a similar scene when things got hectic and when Charlene started coming down with her "drill sergeant" approach.

Charlene finally realized that she was very authoritarian because she had been parented that way herself and that she was making all the rules. She and Dan talked and prayed about their problem and decided to move toward each other in the parenting task rather than farther and farther apart. Charlene learned to ease up and to be more flexible, while Dan learned to take over more when the children caused tension—at the dinner table, for example.

In this way, as a couple they learned to balance out each other's tendencies. Both remained true to who they were but both also grew and became more flexible.

While I've used the example of parenting, the principle applies to other areas as well. One of you might be rigid about making household rules for the other to follow; one of you might be pretty relaxed about establishing routines, which the other desperately needs. One of you might fall in the "miser" category while the other is more of a spendthrift. Marriage brings balance to each of us—if we can just be flexible enough to let it move us from Point A to Point B.

Lord, sometimes our different approaches to life drive us crazy, and we each long for our mate to be just like us. We so soon forget how you work out your perfect purposes in our lives by chipping away our sharp edges and sculpting us into something even more useful and more . . . well, more like you. Help each of us to say, "Break me, mold me, make me a better partner and a better person through the process of living together." Amen.

A Good Match

Gary Smalley

My soul finds rest in God alone; my salvation comes
from him. He alone is my rock and my salvation; he is my
fortress, I will never be shaken.

PSALM 62:1–2

Recently, I received a card in the mail from my wife. In it, she said that she loved me, that every year of our marriage was more fulfilling, and that she appreciated some of my recent attitudes and actions. There wasn't a whiff of hidden expectations in the card. She didn't ask for a thing, but she sure made me want to do more for her.

Through the years, Norma's "no beg" attitude has inspired me to search for creative ways to express my love to her. And it all started with some tattered furniture in our marriage's early years.

Norma was sick and tired of the pitiful "late garage-sale" furniture we owned. For months she asked me to replace it. "Gary, it's just awful. I'm so embarrassed when our friends come over, we need to get new furniture!"

I felt like a slave to her expectations. *No matter what I do, she'll never be satisfied,* I thought. *I'm not about to buy her any new furniture with that attitude!* (What a domineering spirit I had then.)

Then one day it dawned on me: She hadn't said a word about that furniture for more than a year. She hadn't even dropped hints. When I asked her about it, I found out that she had given up her expectations to the Lord (Psalm 62:1–2). She had chosen to focus on God-filled happiness rather than stuff-filled happiness.

At that moment I was willing to do anything for her. I even asked her how much money she would like to withdraw from our savings account for new furniture. Then we marched down to the local furniture store and bought a couch, lamps, tables, chairs. Of course, after we purchased all the furniture, we couldn't afford a house to put it in, but Norma was as happy as a bee discovering a flower-filled plant—and so was I.

Norma's initial complaints accomplished nothing, but her undemanding patience accomplished everything. Around our house we've noticed several factors that make it easier for any family member to change: expressing the change you desire to see without attaching a time limit; showing appreciation for the slightest move toward change; and showing acceptance and love regardless of change.

Norma taught me a lot through that experience, including that her patient approach can win over even someone as stubborn as I was. And that we were a good match for each other— Norma with her consistent, quiet, loving approach, and me, with my all-or-nothing loving approach.

> Lord, loosen our grip on the things that we think we need to make our life together happy. Then fill our open hands with the things you know we need. Amen.

In an
Understanding
Way

Paul Johnson

Husbands, in the same way be considerate as you live
with your wives, and treat them with respect as the weaker
partner and as heirs with you of the gracious gift of life,
so that nothing will hinder your prayers.

1 PETER 3:7

Nicole and I perform a dramatic sketch that is a Scripture medley on marriage and loving one another. We draw primarily from Genesis 2 and 1 Corinthians 13, with a scattering of verses from Proverbs and Song of Songs. Well, 1 Peter 3:7 found its way into the piece, but the translation we use says, "Live with your wives in an understanding way."

Huh? Excuse me, but what exactly is that? Somehow, I don't think the New International translation of "be considerate" means simply to "be nice" to your wife. "Live with your wives in an understanding way." I have one question: Is that possible?

Kevin Leman has mentioned many times as he talks at the Couples of Faith conferences that our wives want us men to read their minds—to automatically know where they want to go out to eat, to compliment their appearance without being prompted, to pick out something they would consider a perfect gift.

I confess, fear strikes my heart when I'm going out just to pick up some lunch for us and I ask Nicole what she would like to eat, and she says, "Surprise me." No-o-o-o! How can I read her mind? I can't even decipher what's in *my* mind.

Hmm, maybe that's part of the problem. On most days, I don't understand myself—what I want, how I feel, how I'm operating, how what I do or say affects another person. I'm much more comfortable having a list handed to me, being told, "Do this today," and doing it. Without thinking, just doing it. We men experience a certain level of comfort when we can operate without thinking. Why is watching sports such a priority? No thinking is required, just watching.

I'm uncomfortable when called on to consider the deeper questions of who I am and what I want of myself. It takes several moments for me to know how to respond to such ponderous questions as "What are you feeling?" or "What did you think about what just happened?" Huh?

Nicole, on the other hand, can say with due speed what she's feeling and thinking now, then, and possibly tomorrow. How does she do that? (I think it's in part because she's willing to be aware.)

I belong to a men's group. We often are asked to express our feelings about what another man is saying. Countless times I've heard a guy say, "I don't know. I'm just a simple guy. I don't understand such things." I've heard myself say that. And I see that it's a cop-out. It's not that I don't understand; it's that I'm unwilling to take the time to live with the feeling long enough to understand what it is and how I react to it. But there is such power when I do, when I see the feelings and thoughts being generated within me by another person and then respond to that person in a truthful yet dignified manner. It takes work (which I loathe), but the result is powerful and enriching (which I love).

As men, we are called to be complex creatures, to utilize our hearts as well as our bodies and our minds. To do more than function without thought, even though every pore in our bodies cries out, "Leave me alone; it's too much; I'm overloading!" It's far more comfortable to be simple and not contemplate all that happens to us internally. But I'm waking up to the call of God that, as a man, I'm to consider how I affect others and how what they do affects me physically, mentally, emotionally, and spiritually. And the amazing thing is that, as I'm growing in understanding myself, I'm finding myself able to understand Nicole on a deeper level. Amazing.

What if we interpreted the Scripture to read, "Husbands, in the same way be considerate (of who you are) as you live with your wives"? Or "Live with your wives in an understanding way of your own unique ability to affect her and the world"? It's not exactly what the verse was intended to say, but it is something to consider. A man should understand himself and how he relates to the woman God has given him. There is power in living that way. There is hope. And there is life.

Father, show us how to understand ourselves more intricately, to be more self-aware, to be willing to feel—even when those feelings can be kind of scary. Help us to walk in the way you have designed for us—to give of ourselves, to consider who we are, to live out of that awareness, and to sustain our relationships with love, power, and life.

Once home, I announced to Roger that I planned to attend the Advanced CLASS seminar. He calmly reminded me that we didn't have the money for the trip to California, much less for the cost of the conference.

"But, Roger, I know God wants me to go. He has given me a real gift for speaking, and I need to develop it. Won't you pray about letting me go?"

"Becky, I don't need to pray about something we can't afford. We don't have the money, and that's that."

I had heard Roger make similar statements before, so I was not about to give up easily. I decided to go to God in prayer—after all, the Scriptures do say that we are to take our requests to God. And so I did, in full confidence that He would provide.

A few days later, I received an unexpected check in the mail. It was a refund from an overpayment we had made. It was not a fortune, but it was enough to pay for my registration at the conference.

"Roger, look! God has provided the money for the conference!"

"Becky, that money needs to go toward our bills. It's not for a trip to California."

I was disappointed, but I was still determined. I continued to pray, and I continued to believe that somehow God would make a way for me to attend.

Living through a snowy, cloudy winter, I couldn't help but want to leave the area for a few days in the sun. As I drove the two hours home from the seminar and talked aloud to God, I asked him to send me to Advanced CLASS. By the time I pulled into the driveway, I was convinced God wanted me to attend.

After being away for three days, I ran into the house and blurted out to Rog (who had stayed with our four-year-old for seventy-two hours), "Honey, God wants me to go to Advanced CLASS next month in Southern California!"

Without a moment's hesitation, Roger responded, "Well, I don't!"

Pragmatic as ever, he concluded that we didn't have the childcare infrastructure or the extra funds for me to go "gallivanting" across the country. (I also think he was a little sore that I had announced my travel plans before I had even asked him how his weekend with Jacob had gone.)

Well, I was dejected. We were a family that prayed about the decisions we made, and whenever Earth-to-Mars Roger tried to communicate, and I didn't want to hear—or vice versa—we chose to pray harder, differently, more specifically. So I began to pray and ask God to show me if I was just being selfish or impulsive, or if, in fact, he wanted me to go to California. After a few days, I still felt strongly that God wanted me to go, so I asked Roger, "What would God have to do to show you that he *did* want me to go to CLASS next month?"

Reliable Roger replied, "He'd have to pay your way."

Needless to say, that's the way the dreamer in me began to pray. So every day, I would ask God, "If you want me to go, would you pay my way?"

A few weeks before the registration deadline, I received a phone call from the CLASS office. After a few questions regarding my desire to come but my inability to pay, the CLASS representative said, "Becky, someday I believe you will come to Advanced CLASS."

Ten minutes later, he called me back and said, "Becky, God has impressed on my heart to offer you a scholarship to attend CLASS next month."

I screamed into the phone, "He did it!" Then I told the man that I would have to call him back after speaking about the offer with my husband.

I ran into the living room and yelled, "Honey, you won't believe what God did—and he even paid my way!"

Though I had to overcome several obstacles to attend the event, I look back and am certain Roger and I were supposed to prayerfully persevere through our differences of opinion. I'm grateful that, when Roger and I don't initially agree on some big or small decision, we have made it part of our conflict management to talk to God and ask him to show us his plan for our lives. We both have found this principle in the book of James practical and powerful: "If any of you lacks wisdom, he should ask God, who gives generously to all without finding fault, and it will be given to him."

So it was on that day that Pragmatic Roger and Fanciful Becky both got their wish. And God showed us how we balance one another, Roger keeping hold of the string on my balloon, as the balloon pulls him up—just a little bit—toward the sky.

Lord, keep us open to your will for our lives. Give us wisdom and direction. Help us to trust you when we don't agree with each other. Help us to wait for your plan to unfold but not to be afraid to move forward when you show us your timing. Enable us to see how we balance one another—the dreamer and the realist—and how you brought us together. Amen.

Destination Joy

Nicole Johnson

You have made known to me the path of life;
you will fill me with joy in your presence.

PSALM 16:11

The day was beautiful, bright, and clear with a touch of crisp fall air. We set out on one of our favorite Saturday afternoon excursions: a movie. The car windows were down, and the breeze was glorious. We were listening to football on the radio and chatting about our expectations for the upcoming flick. We were ten minutes away from the theater when the traffic on the freeway came to a stop, along with our conversation.

Paul sighed in deep frustration.

I waited, knowing what was coming.

"Why does this always happen to us?" he demanded, taking his first step toward Grumpyland.

"This doesn't always happen to us," I answered, trying to set up a detour.

"Yes, it does. Every time I want to go somewhere, I get stuck in this stupid construction traffic. We're going to miss the movie." Paul proceeded to pound on the steering wheel in frustration—a tactic known to speed up traffic just like pushing an elevator button in rapid succession speeds up its arrival.

"We aren't going to miss the movie," I said in my best, everything-is-going-to-be-fine voice, knowing that we were probably going to miss the movie. "Maybe just a few previews," I threw in to prepare our hearts for disappointment.

"I knew we should have left earlier."

Ah, the "I can't do anything about this, but I'll feel better by blaming you" approach. I was having none of it. "This doesn't happen to us every time, and even if we miss the movie, we don't have to let it wreck the day."

He stared at me as if I had two heads. "If we miss the movie, the day is wrecked."

I realized then that we had different destinations. He was going to a movie, I was going to a good time. There is a difference. One destination is not better than the other, and on good days they are the same thing. But this day, when traffic came to a stop, our destinations parted ways. Paul wanted to see a movie; so the traffic was blocking his goal. I wanted to have a good time, and Paul's attitude was blocking my goal. I didn't care if we went to a movie or Thailand; I was enjoying the conversation and connection so the traffic didn't bother me.

He continued to fume and fuss and weasel his way onto the shoulder of the interstate toward his goal. I tried to be light and funny. His jaw was set, and he was mad. The angrier he became at the traffic, the angrier I became at his mood. Neither of us was going to get where we wanted to go.

"Why aren't you having fun?" I asked.

"I'll start having fun when we get there," he answered.

"But I want to have fun on the way, or I won't have fun when we get there."

We blazed a new trail to the theater. (It's a good thing we didn't have to get home the same way, or we'd have been sorry we hadn't left breadcrumbs.) Paul drove like a maniac. When we arrived and settled into our seats, only having missed a few previews, Paul was happy. I was miserable. We had fought for the last twenty minutes, blaming each other, while Paul put our lives in danger with his driving. Now I was frustrated and crabby. I couldn't enjoy the movie. Paul was happy as a clam.

In the Christian life, what is the destination? Our answer to that question will determine how we live out our faith. If the destination is heaven, then we may not pay much attention to how we live here on earth. If the destination is becoming more Christlike and heaven is after that, then how we live matters a lot. We find ourselves more involved in the process than the product. How we get there is as important to some as getting there. Having joy, peace, and other fruits of the Spirit don't just happen when we get to heaven; they happen now, along the way.

Some people focus on the destination. Others focus on the journey. Usually God puts one of each in a marriage. Maybe he does that so we don't forget that both are important. Maybe he wants us to find a good mix of process and product. If we don't enjoy the journey, we might not enjoy the destination, and if we don't keep our eyes on the destination, the journey becomes the end in itself, which isn't the way God intended. The goal of school isn't school—it's graduation; that's the destination. But just to graduate isn't the goal either; it's to learn.

A movie with an angry wife isn't fulfilling. No movie but a happy wife isn't what Paul wanted either. Learning to mix the journey and the destination is the secret of the Christian life— setting our sights on heaven and finding joy on earth.

Someone should make a movie about that. I'd go.

Father, don't let us set our sights on the wrong destination. Keep us focused on where we're going but not to the exclusion of how we treat others along the way. Remind us of your love in the process, that we might find joy in the journey and hope in the eternal destination. Thank you for life's traffic jams that force us to stop long enough to recognize truth that we wouldn't see otherwise. Amen.

Part Eight
Celebrating Romance and Passion

THE NAKED LADY WHO NEEDED A LIFT

Dr. Kevin Leman

My lover is mine and I am his.

SONG OF SONGS 2:16

I f anything kills romance, it's sameness. Every married couple experiences the letdown that follows the breathlessness of falling in love and tying the knot. That's when they discover that reality seems to leave out romance. But it doesn't have to be that way if you're both committed to keeping each other off balance with little surprises that say in different ways, "I love you," "I'm proud of you," "I really like being married to you!" And sometimes the surprises can be big ones—wild and crazy stuff.

One of the more outstanding examples of the wild and crazy possibilities involves a couple I counseled whose marriage had gotten into the sexual doldrums. During a counseling session I had alone with the wife, I mentioned to her that sometimes it really helps when the woman is more aggressive and takes a more active role in initiating sex.

I never cease to marvel at what people can do with a simple suggestion.

Not many days later, this couple went to a party. Due to their busy schedules, they had to drive separately. As the party ended, the wife managed to leave before the husband. She arrived home several minutes ahead of him at the long, common driveway they shared with the family who lived next door. After going down the pavement almost a quarter of a mile, she pulled off to the side and removed every stitch of her clothing.

In a few minutes, she saw headlights turn into the driveway, and she climbed out of her car and stood there, stark naked, with her thumb out as if she were hitchhiking. As the headlights approached, it occurred to her she hadn't reached the Y in the driveway, with one part leading to her house and the other to the neighbor's. *What if this isn't my husband? What if it's the neighbor instead?*

By then it was too late. The headlights caught her in their glare, the car stopped, and the door opened. Fortunately, it was her husband, who went along with the gag and asked, "Hey, lady, do you need a lift?"

Hitchhiking naked and hoping your husband comes along first may not be your style, but you can do other little crazy things. A friend of mine came home from work and found his wife on the dresser ready to leap into his arms. This wasn't exactly typical behavior, but even more unusual than the dresser-top perch was the way she had dressed for the occasion—in nothing but Saran Wrap.

"Kevin, if you think getting Saran Wrap off a sweaty body is easy, just try it sometime!" he said. Then he admitted he had a lot of fun seeing how long it would take him to peel off the Saran Wrap.

Needless to say, the willingness to do something wild and crazy gave the love lives of both of these women a lift. I've seen it happen many times. When a woman becomes assertive and aggressive sexually with her husband, it does wonders for his self-esteem, and it puts her more in the mood for lovemaking.

On the other side of the coin, when a man tones down his natural male aggressiveness and gently centers his thoughts on pleasing his wife, she becomes more interested in sex and possibly becomes more aggressive herself. So turn up your Romantic Notions buttons and stay tuned for what happens next.

Lord, thank you for the gifts of creativity and humor. Help us to use both of these qualities to bring spontaneity, fun, and memorable moments into our relationship.

Mystery Solved

Gary Smalley

*In your anger do not sin: Do not let the sun go
down while you are still angry.*

EPHESIANS 4:26

At 4:00 P.M. on Valentine's Day I remembered my basketball game. I reached for the phone to call Norma, my bride of less than a year. "Honey, I forgot to tell you I have to play basketball tonight. We're supposed to be there about seven. I'll pick you up about 6:30."

Silence hung heavily on the line before she answered, "But this is Valentine's Day."

"Yeah, I know, but I need to be there tonight. I don't want to let the team down."

"But I have a special dinner prepared with candles and—"

"Can you hold it off until tomorrow?" She didn't answer, so I continued. "Honey, you know how important it is for a wife to submit to her husband. I really need to be at the game tonight, and if we're going to start off with good habits in the early part of our marriage, now is the time to begin. If I'm going to be the leader of the family, I need to make the decision."

Like many young husbands, I didn't have a clue how deeply my comments wounded Norma. I didn't know it, but I had just caused serious damage to our relationship.

"Ice" describes the reception I received when I picked her up. It was easy to see I had offended her, but I figured she had to learn submissiveness sometime, and we might as well start now. The lifeless expression on her face grew worse as the evening wore on.

When we returned home after the game, I noticed the table was set up for a special dinner—candles, our best dishes, and pretty napkins. Now, you would think it wouldn't take a Sherlock Holmes to figure out I had punctured the balloon of romance, but, hey, I never claimed to be a detective.

She still wasn't speaking to me the next day, so I did have enough sense to rush to the florist where I gathered a variety of flowers, which I put in various spots around the house. That warmed her up a little. Then I gave her a giant card with a hand on the front that could be turned thumbs up or thumbs down. "Which way is it?" I asked her.

She turned it thumbs up. I never said whether I was right or wrong, only that I felt bad about the night before. And so began a history of offenses I didn't know how to clear up with her. Had someone not shared with me later the secret of developing a lasting and intimate relationship, Norma and I might have joined the millions who seek divorce each year.

Couples often ask me, "Where have we gone wrong?" "Why don't we feel romantic toward each other?" "How come we argue so much?" These problems usually aren't attributable to incompatibility, sexual problems, financial pressure, or any other surface issue. They are a direct result of accumulated offenses. If a husband and wife can understand how to maintain harmony by immediately working to clear up every hurtful offense between them, they can climb out of such common problems and every marriage's deepest pit—divorce. Romance returns and passion is ignited. I might not be Sherlock, but I have managed to figure all this out, thanks in large part to Norma.

Love and romance aren't about whether or not I should have gone to the basketball game. They're about recognizing when I hurt my mate's feelings and then asking how I can repair them. Without the "guilty party" confessing and asking pardon, it doesn't matter if it's Valentine's Day, your anniversary, or any other day that naturally tilts toward romance. You're going straight to jail, buddy, and you won't get to pass "go," believe me.

Lord, teach us to face our offenses toward one another honestly and to confess our wrongdoing openly. Help us to turn our passion to expressions of love rather than anger. And remind both of us how quickly the light of passion can be extinguished by hurts not dealt with. Amen.

Love, Sex, and the Church Lady?

Les and Leslie Parrott

> Then the LORD God made a woman from the rib he had
> taken out of the man, and he brought her to the man. The
> man said, "This is now bone of my bones and flesh of my flesh;
> she shall be called 'woman,' for she was taken out of man." For this
> reason a man will leave his father and mother and be united
> to his wife, and they will become one flesh. The man and his
> wife were both naked, and they felt no shame.
>
> GENESIS 2:22–25

Sigmund Freud said they suffer from "obsessional neurosis" accompanied by guilt, suppressed emotions, and repressed sexuality. Former *Saturday Night Live* comedian Dana Carvey satirized them as uptight prudes who believe sex is downright dirty. But several major research studies have shown that church ladies, as well as their husbands, are among the most sexually satisfied people on the face of the earth. Researchers at the University of Chicago recently released the results of the most "comprehensive and methodologically sound" sex survey ever conducted.

They reported that religious women experience significantly higher levels of sexual satisfaction than non-religious women.

While this outcome caught some by surprise, the Chicago study was hardly the first to show a link between spirituality and sexuality. As far back as the 1940s, researchers have found higher levels of sexual satisfaction among women who attend religious services religiously.

So, with these scientific findings in mind, the question is what are you doing about it? In other words, how's your sex life? The mysteries, wonders, and pleasures of sex in marriage are a divine gift to celebrate. Those who try to limit sex to procreation are simply ignoring the Bible. Scripture—right from the beginning—enthusiastically affirms sex within the bonds of marriage.

Start with the Bible's first chapter. It contains a magnificent comment on the meaning of sexuality in marriage. As God brings the universe into existence, we are told that the human creation is set apart from all others, for it is the *imago Dei*, the image of God. "So God created man in his own image, in the image of God he created him; male and female he created them" (Genesis 1:27). Our maleness and femaleness are not just an accidental arrangement of the human species. Our male and female sexuality is related to our creation in God's image.

This point is echoed throughout Scripture. Consider the Song of Songs. Karl Barth has called the Song an expanded commentary on Genesis 2:25, "The man and his wife were both naked, and they felt no shame." If Genesis affirms our sexuality, the Song of Songs celebrates it. No other portion of Scripture is more extravagant. The Song of Songs describes sensuality without licentiousness, passion without promiscuity, love without lust.

In the New Testament, Paul quotes the Genesis passage about the husband leaving father and mother and cleaving to his wife so that the two become one flesh, and then Paul adds, "This is a profound mystery—but I am talking about Christ and the church" (Ephesians 5:32).

Jesus, likewise, underscores a high view of marital sex. He refers to the Genesis passage and then says, "So they are no longer two, but one. Therefore what God has joined together, let man not separate" (Matthew 19:6).

In the Old Testament and in the New Testament, in the Gospels and in the Epistles, the call to celebrate sexuality in marriage is found. There's no denying that your spiritual growth helps to enhance your sexual intimacy. So, we'll ask it again: How's your sex life?

> *Father, thank you for the gift of sex in our marriage. And thank you for creating us in a way that brings such ecstasy and physical pleasure with each other. Help us to never take it for granted, and remind us how sexual fulfillment is directly linked to our spiritual lives. Dwell in our marriage. Enhance our oneness in body and soul. Amen.*

Praying
Together

Gary Smalley

But I pray to you, O LORD, in the time of your favor;
in your great love, O God, answer me
with your sure salvation.

PSALM 69:13

Often we have an unbalanced view of what intimacy is and
how it manifests itself in marriage. There are really two
sides to intimacy between a husband and a wife: the physical and
the emotional.

Prayer is a great way to build emotional intimacy into your
marriage. Many times we don't know how to pray so we allow
this to keep us from a life of prayer, especially with our spouse.
So I'd like to explain the elements of a healthy prayer life using
my youngest son's experience as an example.

Michael always longed to be married. He used to tell me,
even in elementary school, that he wanted to be married before
he graduated from college. I never gave this adamantly
expressed marital interest much thought. But something hap-

pened his junior year in college that made me realize how serious he was.

Apparently Michael had been praying fervently for a wife, and he had a specific girl in mind. During his freshman year at Baylor University he had met Amy, one of Baylor's cheerleaders, during her tryout to make the squad. Amy had left such an impression on my son that he actually trained to become a cheerleader himself. (Baylor had men and women as cheerleaders.) The next year he tried out for the squad and made the team—all this just to get closer to Amy, whom he had barely spoken to!

My son's personality is such that he doesn't always check out all the facts. (Wonder who he inherited that trait from . . .) In his zeal to make the team, he had forgotten to check if Amy was dating anyone seriously. As it turned out, she was engaged.

Michael was devastated and spent the next two years of college as just a friend to Amy. But during that time Michael developed some good prayer habits.

To Michael, Amy was the ideal woman. She had everything he could hope for in a wife, and quite frankly, he couldn't imagine finding a better woman to marry. Considering that she was engaged to another man, Michael's prayer went something like this: "God, you know who my heart wants to marry. I'm not going to lie or try to feel something different. I want to marry Amy. But if Amy isn't the one, I can't wait to meet the girl I will marry, because I know that she will be even better!"

What can you, as a couple, learn about prayer from Michael? First, we must pray for what we desire. God knows all our thoughts, feelings, and beliefs. Why try to fool God or ourselves? Too often we pray for things we don't hunger for. God wants us to be real, and being real means being truthful. Michael wanted to marry Amy, even though she was engaged. That didn't stop him from praying for her and their potential future together.

The second part, and perhaps the most important, was that Michael was willing to accept God's will, even if it didn't match his own. That attitude is expressed when you add to the end of your prayer something like, "But God, if this isn't what you want for me, then I can't wait to find out what your plan is." We must wait in anticipation of God's fulfillment of our prayer, knowing that God's way is the best way.

By applying those two principles to your prayer time with your spouse, you're experiencing open communication, open hearts, and souls ready to receive what God chooses to give. I can't imagine a better formula for emotional intimacy.

Oh, by the way, Michael did end up marrying Amy. But that's another story.

> *Lord, help us to faithfully develop a prayer life together in which we honestly express how we feel, lay our dreams before you, and wait expectantly for what you'll send our way. Our heart's desire is to talk with you, walk with you, and be with you—together.*

WILDCAT AND ZUCCHINI SMORGASBORD

Dr. Kevin Leman

*So in everything, do to others what you would
have them do to you, for this sums up
the Law and the Prophets.*

MATTHEW 7:12

This may come as a surprise to you, but I think one of the most romantic things a couple can do for each other is to, well, "do for each other." In other words, spend time at some recreational activity the other person really cares about, even if you don't understand why all the fuss.

Tucson, where Sande and I live, is a cow town that made good and happily became the home of the University of Arizona. But Tucson isn't exactly the center of the universe when it comes to professional sports, stage shows, or other forms of big city entertainment. So it's easy to understand why the University of Arizona Wildcats are the only game in town. As an alumnus of the U of A, as well as an avid sports fan, I hold a season ticket for all the football and basketball games. Rain or shine, win or lose, you'll find Leman and his family out there singing the Arizona fight song and urging our Cats to "bear down!"

Sande has faithfully attended these games with me for years, even though she is hardly a sports fan. I'm fairly sure that, if Sande had her druthers, she wouldn't attend another football or basketball game her entire life. Nonetheless, she's there with me because she knows I like her to be.

I call that "recreational companionship," which to me means doing different things together or, for even more fun, doing things together differently. At a lot of football games, Sande and I go together, but we certainly wind up doing things differently. I sit there screaming for the Cats as they make a goal-line stand, and I look over at Sande to see her flipping through, of all things, a recipe book. The pure and simple truth is that she loves to read recipes, and when she tires of the game, she whips out her latest collection to see what she can find. So there we are: I'm wondering why the Cats don't try an end run, and she's contemplating zucchini au gratin.

While Sande goes to my games, I go with her to antique shops. As you might guess, I'm not really into antiques, but it's one of Sande's favorite sports. During our summers back in western New York State, she loves to prowl old and dusty antique shops on the back roads, and that's where we can be found on many a hot summer day.

And you know what? When we come home from those events we've shared together, we feel closer to one another, and that feels downright romantic to both of us.

> Lord, help us to learn to share our different interests and to do things differently together whenever possible. Remind each of us that shared moments lead to a special kind of closeness. Enable us to know how to compromise when our interests would take us in different directions. Above all, help us to use our interests to join us together rather than separating us. Amen.

He Shoots,
He Misses . . .
But Can He Recover?

Les and Leslie Parrott

*May your fountain be blessed, and may you
rejoice in the wife of your youth.*

Proverbs 5:18

We had just flown into Lexington, Kentucky, for a speaking engagement the next morning. But the night was young so we headed to the nicest restaurant we could find. Just the two of us. It would be a quiet, romantic evening to allow our souls to catch up.

We studied the menu and eventually placed our orders. "I'll be right back," Les told me. "I just want to check my voice mail at the office."

I didn't say a word, but he could read the disappointment on my face. "It won't take long," he said as he sheepishly headed to the pay phone.

When Les returned, I had completed my salad and was beginning my entree. His salad sat untouched at his place setting. "Wow, that was fast," he said, sliding into the booth and arranging his linen napkin.

"Fast?" I said sarcastically. "You've been gone for twenty minutes."

After we argued about the length of time Les had been gone from the table, he eventually owned up. "You're right. I was insensitive to leave you here, and I'm so sorry I've spoiled our romantic evening."

That simple apology saved the dying embers of romance. Thankfully, I decided to excuse his lengthy exit, and that was enough to turn our evening around. It ended up being one of the most enjoyable evenings we had had together in a long time. Not that it was the ideal of romance either of us would have pictured, but it was romantic nonetheless.

What's your picture of an ideal day or night of romance? Survey results reveal that many of us would like breakfast in bed, a picnic in the country, or an elegant dinner. A Jacuzzi figures prominently in some responses. A lot of people like the surprise factor. But one of the most common responses is the absence of interruptions. One woman spoke for many when she said her ideal day of romance was that her husband didn't call his office or take calls on his portable phone. (Too bad Les didn't hear about that before our trip to Lexington.)

The message is clear, men. You don't have to be a Mel Gibson or a Brad Pitt to make an evening with your partner exciting. You don't have to spend money like Donald Trump to be romantic. Women aren't necessarily looking for expensive, pre-programmed evenings. They will take the spontaneous, heartfelt gesture of love every time.

So I ask you husbands: What are you doing to rejoice in the wife of your youth? Remember her? She's the woman with whom you patiently picked out a china pattern before you got married. The woman for whom you wrote poetry or planned a surprise trip to the zoo. The woman who took priority over every work deadline and all other appointments. This is the wife of your youth. Remember?

And I ask you wives: What are you doing to rejoice in the husband of your youth? Remember him? He's the man, before you married, that you happily tagged along with to check out the latest in pickup trucks. The man for whom you cooked exquisite meals (with candlelight). The man for whom you carefully picked out what you would wear before each big date. The man you talked about incessantly to your friends, managing to find a connection between any conversational topic and how wonderful he was. This is the husband of your youth. Remember?

And according to Proverbs, it's time you got reacquainted. Listen to these wise words from Solomon: "A wife of noble character who can find? She is worth far more than rubies. Her husband has full confidence in her and lacks nothing of value. She brings him good, not harm, all the days of her life" (Proverbs 31:10–12). And the same goes for husbands.

Let's be honest. If we have found a noble wife or husband, we are blessed. And it's time to rejoice in our blessing.

Heavenly Father, you know how often we mess up a perfectly good evening together because one of us does something insensitive. We may not mean to hurt each other, but it happens. Help each of us to be courageous enough to step beyond our partner's romantic foibles. Help us to give one another grace, just as you have given it to us. Amen.

Sign
and
Stuff

Paul Johnson

> *You are a garden locked up, my sister, my bride;*
> *you are a spring enclosed, a sealed fountain.*
> *Your plants are an orchard of pomegranates with*
> *choice fruits, with henna and nard.*

SONGS OF SONGS 4:12–13

When I was a kid, my mother bought my valentines for me. I would just sign them and stuff them into the other kids' sacks at school. Even the special one that went to the girl I thought was the cutest—sign and stuff. No thinking, really. Not much planning, just sign and stuff.

Well, those days are long gone. Not only is there no more signing and stuffing, but my mother wouldn't think of helping me pick out a card for Nicole. Nor would I want her to because I know Nicole wants me to do it. But as an adult male, picking out the right anything for a woman is tricky.

Where does a guy go for help? Naturally I think of the Song of Songs. But this book in the Bible mocks me. I think it mocks most men. If it really is the book of the Bible that reveals the most about a romantic relationship, I'm in big trouble. I don't know what half of that stuff is, and frankly, I'm scared of it. Garments that smell like Lebanon, noses like towers, and what is "nard" anyway? Where do you get it and what do you do with it once you find it? My best guess is that it's a bath product, or good-smelling something. But if it's that important, it needs a little broader distribution to make sure men can find it. Like put it at the checkout line at Home Depot, next to the flame-throwers.

When it comes to romance, I've found unspoken expectations dot the landscape of a relationship like land mines. I've worked my way around a few close ones, but I'll admit, I've spent the better part of twelve years of marriage hitting those mines and then marking an X on the map. Then I remember that land mines you can mark, but lightning never strikes twice in the same place.

I want to be more romantic. Actually, I want Nicole to think I'm more romantic. The truth is, when you don't really understand what makes something romantic and what doesn't, you can't cultivate it very well. It's a mystery to me, like nard. I mean, I can plunk down fifty dollars for a meal and a movie, and on the way home, Nicole tells me she wants more romance. But when I locked the keys in the car, and we had to walk two miles in pouring rain to a pay phone, she told me, "You're so romantic!" That inspired me to lock the keys in the car the next week on purpose; it didn't work like I'd hoped. Very confusing.

Nard aside, I have discovered one thing about romance: It must be personal. All the "romance" in the world won't mean a thing to my wife if it doesn't come from me. I know it's strange, but she would rather have my awkward, three-line poem than a beautiful, frilly card quoting Wordsworth. Unless the beautiful, frilly card really expresses what I want to say, and I have intentionally picked it out for its special meaning. Then I still have to personalize it. She doesn't want anything close to sign and stuff. Or the nard, until I know what it is.

Romance is the electricity around intimacy. Intimacy happens when people give of themselves in a way that is unique and personal. Ever notice that when you eat out together and you have a special time, then that restaurant takes on special significance in your relationship? Or when you were dating, you and your spouse had "your song"? Those restaurants and songs weren't the only ones out there, but because they were used to bring you closer, they became endowed with special meaning. They became personal.

Women love all those personal touches, and men do, too. We were created to be in deeply personal relationships because we were created by a relational God. While the Song of Songs depicts what Solomon thinks of love and romance, it also reveals God's longing to relate to us. The Creator of the universe is a personal God. He desires to connect with us intimately. He has reservations for us at places that we enjoy, and he knows our favorite songs.

When it came time for him to demonstrate his love, he didn't just sign and stuff. Instead, he carefully crafted what he wanted to say. And he delivered it in the most personal way through Jesus Christ.

In romance, it doesn't matter so much what you do, as long as you know why you're doing it. If I pick up some candles at a local shop because I know Nicole likes candles, I also know she doesn't care if they're beet-scented or lavender. She knows I know her. And that's what she longs for. She wants to feel known. It's what we all long for. But that feeling doesn't occur when I just scribble my name across a piece of paper, or put a gift under the tree that I picked up rather than picked out. The secret of romance lies in making things personal.

Of course, it wouldn't hurt to offer a few of those personal touches at Home Depot.

> *Lord, give us a true taste of a personal relationship with you so that we might understand how to better love our spouses. We confess in our confusion we often give up and don't love them well at all. Forgive us for the times we've "signed and stuffed" and not brought our full hearts to you or to them. Teach us how to love personally.*

About
the Authors

Dr. Larry and Rachael Crabb

Psychologist, speaker, Bible teacher, and author, Dr. Larry Crabb also currently is professor and distinguished scholar in residence at Colorado Christian University. Dr. Crabb has authored many best-selling books, including *Understanding People*, *The Marriage Builder*, *Inside Out*, *Finding God*, and *Connecting*. His newest book is *The Safest Place on Earth*.

Rachael Crabb taught elementary school in Champaign, Illinois, and holds a master's degree in early childhood education. She is the author of *The Personal Touch*, a NavPress publication, and serves on the advisory board of MOPS International (Mothers of Preschoolers) and as a consultant for Stonecroft Ministries (Christian Women's Club). She has spoken for conferences, retreats, and banquets worldwide.

The Crabbs reside in Colorado and have two sons and one granddaughter. They can be contacted at

Dr. Larry and Rachael Crabb
2201 West Dry Creek Road
Littleton, CO 80120
(303) 730-7172
Web site: www.larrycrabb-ibc.com

PAUL AND NICOLE JOHNSON

Since 1988, Paul and Nicole Johnson have brought their original drama to more than a million people through appearances on such national television programs as *Crook & Chase*, *The 700 Club*, and *Life Today with James Robison* and on radio programs such as *Family Life Today*, *Focus on the Family with James Dobson*, and *Midday Connection*. They have been featured on the covers of *Marriage Partnership*, *Focus on the Family*, *Today's Christian Woman*, and *Home Life* magazines. The Johnsons also perform at conferences, including "Couples of Faith," Gary Smalley's "Love Is a Decision," Focus on the Family's "Life on the Edge," and "Aspiring Women."

Their latest projects include *Fresh Brewed Life: A Stirring Invitation to Wake Up Your Soul*, by Nicole, published by Thomas Nelson, and the video, "Vive La Difference: Improving Your Marriage by Embracing the Uniqueness of Your Spouse," produced by Focus on the Family Films.

They can be contacted at

> Johnson Creative Enterprises, Inc.
> P.O. Box 3027
> Brentwood, TN 37027
> (615) 661-0220
> Web site: www.paulandnicole.com

DR. KEVIN LEMAN

An internationally known psychologist, author, and speaker, Dr. Kevin Leman has made house calls via numerous television programs, including *Oprah*, *CBS This Morning*, *Live with Regis and Kathie Lee*, *The Today Show*, and *The View with Barbara Walters*. He has served as a consulting family psychologist to *Good Morning America* and is the host of the television program *RealFAMILIES*. Dr. Leman also is the founder and president of Couples of Promise, an organization designed to help couples remain happily married. His seventeen books include such best-sellers as *The New Birth Order Book, Making Children Mind Without Losing Yours,* and *Becoming a Couple of Promise.*

He received his bachelor's degree in psychology from the University of Arizona as well as his master's and doctorate. He and his wife, Sande, live in Tucson with their five children. He can be reached through his Web site, couplesofpromise.com, or by phoning his office at (520) 797-3830.

DRS. LES AND LESLIE PARROTT

The Parrotts serve as codirectors of the Center for Relationship Development, a groundbreaking program dedicated to teaching the basics of good relationships. Les also teaches psychology at Seattle Pacific University, and Leslie is a marriage and family therapist on the campus.

They have written *Becoming Soul Mates, The Marriage Mentor Manual, Questions Couples Ask, Meditations on Proverbs for Couples, Getting Ready for the Wedding, A Good Friend, Relationships, Love Is,* and the award-winning *Saving Your Marriage Before It Starts.*

They have appeared on *CNN, Today, Good Morning America, Nightly News with Tom Brokaw, The View with Barbara Walters,* and *Oprah.*

Their Web site is www.RealRelationships.com

GARY SMALLEY

Gary Smalley is the author and coauthor of sixteen bestselling, award-winning books along with several popular films and videos. His books have sold more than five million copies, with *The Blessing* and *The Two Sides of Love* winning the Gold Medallion. *The Language of Love* won the Angel Award, and all his other titles have been Gold Medallion finalists.

Having spoken to more than two million people in live conferences, Gary also has appeared on such television programs as

Oprah, Larry King Live, Extra, The Today Show, and *Sally Jessie Raphael.* Gary's son, Michael, adapted several of his father's messages into devotionals for this book.

Gary and his wife, Norma, have been married thirty-five years and have three children and six grandchildren. Their ministry can be reached at

> Smalley Relationship Center
> 1482 Lakeshore Dr.
> Branson, MO 65616
> (417) 335-4321
> Web site: smalleyrelationships.com

BECKY AND ROGER TIRABASSI

Becky and Roger Tirabassi have been married for more than twenty-two years. Their son, Jacob, has left the nest to attend college.

Becky is a motivational speaker and author of the best-selling books *Let Prayer Change Your Life* and *My Partner Prayer Notebook.* Her newest release is *Change Your Life: Achieve a Healthy Body, Heal Your Relationships, and Connect with God* (Putnam).

Roger is a pastoral counselor who specializes in encouraging engaged and married couples to love God and each other. He has a master's in counseling and theology and a doctorate in ministry.

Together, they have coauthored *How to Live with Them, Since You Can't Live without Them* (Thomas Nelson).

You can contact them at

> Becky Tirabassi Change Your Life Inc.™
> Box 9672
> Newport Beach, CA 92660
> 1-800-444-6189
> Web site: www.changeyourlifedaily.com

Dr. Neil Clark Warren

As one of America's best-known relational psychologists, Dr. Warren earned his Master of Divinity degree from Princeton Theological Seminary and his Ph.D. in clinical psychology from the University of Chicago.

His first book, *Make Anger Your Ally*, was heralded a "must read" by *Time* magazine, and his best-selling *Finding the Love of Your Life* won a Gold Medallion. *Learning to Live with the Love of Your Life, and Loving It* was selected by *USA Today* as an outstanding contribution to the field of marriage. His most recent books are *God Said It, Don't Sweat It* and *How to Know If Someone Is Worth Pursuing in Two Dates or Less*.

Dr. Warren has appeared on such shows as *Oprah, Geraldo*, and *The 700 Club*.

He and his wife, Marylyn, live in Southern California; they have three grown daughters.

WOMEN OF FAITH^{SM}

Women of Faith partners with various Christian
organizations, including Zondervan Publishing House,
Campus Crusade for Christ International, CleanWeb,
Integrity Music, International Bible Society,
New Life Clinics, New Life Ministries, Partnerships, Inc.,
Power and Glory, Remuda Ranch,
Today's Christian Woman magazine, and
World Vision to provide spiritual resources for women.

For more information about Women of Faith
or to register for one of our nationwide conferences,
call 1-800-49-FAITH.
www.women-of-faith.com

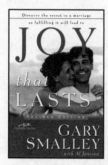

Joy That Lasts
Revised Edition

Gary Smalley with Al Janssen

Is your marriage rich in joy? If not, renowned counselor and author Gary Smalley wants to share five principles that can work wonders for you and your spouse. Smalley knows their effectiveness—the same insights have thoroughly transformed his own marriage. They boil down to what your needs are as individuals and where you're turning to get those needs met. The truth may surprise you. More important, it will change your marriage if you act on it.

Extensively revised to concentrate on the challenges and opportunities of married life, *Joy That Lasts* shows what it means to truly trust God, and how a deep relationship with him can bring the life and joy you long for in your marriage.

Hardcover 0-310-23322-4

We Brake for Joy!

Patsy Clairmont, Barbara Johnson, Marilyn Meberg, Luci Swindoll, Sheila Walsh, and Thelma Wells

Those wild and wonderful women are it again! This book offers 90 upbeat devotions to help you live out your faith with verve and style. Each devotion includes a Scripture passage, a meditation, a closing prayer, and wisdom from traveling companions who know how tough the journey can be—and how good God is.

Hardcover 0-310-22042-4
Audio Pages 0-310-22434-9

Extravagant Grace

**Discover the Grace That Turns
Each Day into a Tale of Transformation**

Patsy Clairmont, Barbara Johnson,
Marilyn Meberg, Luci Swindoll, Sheila
Walsh, and Thelma Wells

Grace that cleanses your sin. Grace that guides your life. Grace
that weathers life's fiercest storms and stamps every cloud with
the rainbow of God's promise. Grace to grieve and laugh, give
and gain, love and live. *Extravagant Grace*.

Here is a devotional filled with laughter as rich as the insights
are deep. With the same wit and insight that have characterized
their previous devotionals such as *Joy Breaks* and *OverJoyed!*
Extravagant Grace celebrates God's liberating power at work in your
circumstances, your relationships, your inner being, your marriage, your vocation, in all the things that matter most to you . . .
and even in things that seem to be of little consequence.

Hardcover 0-310-23125-6
Audio Pages 0310-23126-4

Joy Breaks

Patsy Clairmont, Barbara Johnson,
Marilyn Meberg, and Luci Swindoll

Here are 90 upbeat devotionals that motivate
and support women who want to renew and
deepen their spiritual commitments. Women of
all ages will be reminded that any time, any day,
they can lighten up, get perspective, laugh, and cast all their cares
on the One who cares for them.

Also available is the Joy Breaks Daybreak®, with 128 light-
hearted, inspiring, and joyful devotion excerpts from the book.

Hardcover 0-310-21345-2
Daybreak 0-310-97287-6

OverJoyed!

**Devotions to Tickle Your Fancy
and Strengthen Your Faith**

Patsy Clairmont, Barbara Johnson,
Marilyn Meberg, Luci Swindoll,
Sheila Walsh, and Thelma Wells

What do you get when you mix courage, faith, humor, and a few
spunky women? You get *OverJoyed!*, a devotional by six irrepress-
ible authors who know how to squeeze the maximum amount of
gladness out of life. These 60 sparkling devotions combine fun,
candor, and biblically based wisdom that can help you trade gloom
for glory even in the midst of great adversity.

Hardcover 0-310-22653-8